AUTOGIRO
Pioneer

Jack (right) at Sarzana near La Spezia, in June 1935.

AUTOGIRO
Pioneer
The Life of Jack Richardson

Nicholas Richardson

FONTHILL

This book is dedicated to the memory of the other Autogiro pioneers, and especially Juan de la Cierva y Codorniu, Reggie Brie, Jeep Cable, Alan Marsh, and Yates.

Fonthill Media Language Policy

Fonthill Media publishes in the international English language market. One language edition is published worldwide. As there are minor differences in spelling and presentation, especially with regard to American English and British English, a policy is necessary to define which form of English to use. The Fonthill Policy is to use the form of English native to the author. Nicholas Richardson was born and educated in England; therefore, British English has been adopted in this publication.

Fonthill Media Limited
Fonthill Media LLC
www.fonthillmedia.com
office@fonthillmedia.com

First published in the United Kingdom and the United States of America 2019

British Library Cataloguing in Publication Data:
A catalogue record for this book is available from the British Library

Copyright © Nicholas Richardson 2019

ISBN 978-1-78155-742-6

The right of Nicholas Richardson to be identified as the author of this work has been asserted by him in accordance with the Copyright, Designs and Patents Act 1988.

Typeset in 10pt on 13pt Sabon
Printed and bound in England

Preface

My father's flying career as an Autogiro pioneer, and his later role in the development of the helicopter, will most probably be the main points of interest in his memoirs for some readers. Yet since these memoirs cover his life and family background more generally, I have taken the liberty of including in the notes and appendices a good deal of material relating to these topics. I think that this helps to place his life in a wider context. Needless to say, from a personal point of view, finding out more about this background has itself been a fascinating quest. I must apologise for the fact that some of the results are still fragmentary and leave scope for further investigation.

There are many people whom I wish to thank for their help and advice in the course of work on this book.

Jenny, my wife, first encouraged me to tackle this project and has been a constant support throughout. Our children have all helped in various ways. Alexis alerted me to Autogiro AP507, on display in the Science Museum in London, a machine flown by my father in 1943. Penelope and Andrew gave some advice about the pictures and other technical problems. Catherine has helped a great deal in editing both the pictures and the text, together with Conor Delahunty. I am especially grateful to Conor, who went through all the pictures and made them ready to print, a very considerable task, and who also most generously passed on to me the MacBook Air on which much of the work on this book was done.

For the family background, many cousins have helped in various ways. On the Bishop side, Sue Attwood has been an invaluable source of information, pictures, and encouragement. Gina O'Neill sent me images of some family portraits shortly before she died; her sons, Shane and Tyrone, have been most helpful in taking more photos and sending them to me. Colin Campbell and Willie Stirling located for me the portrait by my grandmother, Mabel, of her sister-in-law, Olive Bishop, and Colin's daughter, Tess, also gave us a friendly welcome, when we found this portrait at her father's home in Dorset. I am very grateful to Prue Hardie and Vicky Kidney, the granddaughters of Vyvien Hart-Davis, for allowing me to include parts of Vyvien's memoirs as an appendix, as well as lending some of their photos. Other cousins who have supplied useful information are John Bishop, Victoria Bishop, and Sarah Hodgson.

On the Richardson side, I must thank David Steel for his excellent family portraits. My half-brother Michael Richardson's daughters, Ann, Mary, and Susan, have all sent me portraits and information about their family. My cousins, Derry and Julian Ormond and Alex Craster, supplied information about the Ormonds, especially as regards the fate of their house in Ciboure during the Second World War.

On my mother's side (the Allan family), my cousin, Penelope Smail, kindly lent me skiing photos that belonged to her mother, Kathleen, my mother's sister.

In the hunt for the two portraits by Henry Tonks of the Bishop sisters (Gladys, Connie, and Vyvien), I am grateful for their advice to Bevis Hillier, Sir Michael Holroyd, Peyton Skipwith, Richard Ormond, and especially to Sabina ffrench-Blake, who is writing a biography of Tonks and has generously given me a great deal of her time and assistance. Thanks are also due to the staff of the Courtauld Institute, for their help in consulting the Witt Collection and using their library. I much regret that so far, I have been unable to track down any reproductions of these paintings or details about their ownership.

The Ventnor Heritage Centre and Museum have useful information about Steephill Castle and the family of John Morgan Richards (the father-in-law of Dorothy Bishop), and I am grateful to the staff there, and also to Michael Freeman, for their advice when we visited it.

Robert Winckworth, at the Archives of University College, London, kindly sent me records of the Slade School, concerning my grandmother, Mabel, and her sisters, Connie and Vyvien.

For information about Vyvien and the Hart-Davis family, I must also thank Duff Hart-Davis; Mrs. B. Dinham and Ann Scourfield (both at Nether Stowey); Mrs Eleanor Hoare, archivist at Eton College; Jennifer Thorp, archivist at New College; and Henrietta Hall, who sent some details about the actresses whom Vyvien helped to dress in 1902–8.

For sailing records of the Richardson family in Glasgow in the late nineteenth century, I must thank Jon Reid, archivist of the Royal Northern Clyde Yacht Club, and Alan Dundas, secretary of the Mudhook Club.

The librarian at Harrow School (Helen) sent details of my father's school record and that of other members of his family.

My former pupil, Richard Hewitt, kindly read the section of the memoirs about farming in Natal and gave me good advice on some of the African details of this.

For the section on skiing, I must thank the staff at the Ski Club of Great Britain for their help in using their invaluable library, and also Tim Ashburner,

John Collard, Jane Fawkes, Maud Instone, Annette Hughes, Ros Humphrey, and Andrew Morgan for details about the early days of skiing and the various ski clubs to which my parents belonged.

Robin Draper kindly lent me books on Gallipoli and alerted me to a talk by Peter Hart on this campaign.

David Twiston-Davies put me in touch with Graham Pitchfork, his colleague on *The Daily Telegraph*. Graham advised me to contact Brian Riddle, the librarian of the National Aerospace Library. His assistance has been invaluable. Thanks to him, I first wrote to Alan Sutton, my publisher, and also made contact with Miss Elizabeth Brie, the daughter of my father's colleague, Reggie Brie. She has been most generous in supplying information about her father's career, checking the sections on flying, and also sending me two pictures from her father's collection. At the outset of this work, I also had some good advice on publishing from Richard Stoneman.

Tony Lawson-Smith's boundless enthusiasm and interest in my father's flying adventures have been a great source of encouragement. I should also like to thank Lydia Segrave (Countess Baldwin) for all the information she gave me about her former husband Ian Little's war career as a rotary-wing test pilot, for which he was awarded the AFC, and Vijay Joshi, who first put me in touch with Lydia.

I am most grateful to Justin Hobson at the Science and Society Picture Library, for supplying the photograph of Autogiro AP507, for waiving their photography fee, and for giving permission to use a photograph of the Cierva C.24 Autogiro (which is owned by the Science Museum). Thanks are due also to the de Havilland Museum (where it is on permanent loan), Alistair Hodgson (the Museum's Curator), and Gary Lakin, for supplying this picture.

Elfan ap Rees kindly gave Jenny and myself a tour of the Helicopter Museum near Weston-super-Mare, which has another Autogiro (G-ACWM), flown by my father in July 1935 and August 1939.

I should like to thank Lucy McCann and Ann Mouron at the Bodleian Library, and the staff of the Radcliffe Science Library in Oxford, for their patient assistance.

Andrea Pass, the copy editor of my last book, most generously read a draft of the memoirs and suggested some corrections.

Finally, I am greatly indebted to Alan Sutton for agreeing to publish this work, and for his very clear instructions and good advice on technical details.

I have dedicated this book to the memory of those courageous Autogiro pilots who were my father's closest colleagues. In the case of Yates, with whom he shared his most hair-raising adventure, the flight to Madrid in midwinter (which involved a forced landing in a bog in the Sierra de Guadarrama), I regret that I have so far been unable to discover any information apart from his surname.

Nicholas Richardson

CONTENTS

Introduction

Sources

During the last few years of his life, my father made several versions of his memoirs. One is a handwritten account, but he also made a series of tape recordings. These often add more details or contain quite new sections, for example about his mother's family. Sometimes, there is more than one tape covering the same material.

I have typed out the written version and have gone through the tapes, making notes and then incorporating the new material from these. In doing so, I kept as closely as possible to his own words, although not always absolutely verbatim.

The resulting text is thus a composite version of these sources. Sometimes, the written account differs over details from the tapes. It has often been possible to check names, dates, etc., but occasionally, I could not verify which version was correct.

As he says himself, his cousin, Kitty Richardson, put together an excellent history of his father's family, and so he does not say a great deal about this. I have also checked some points with cousins on this side, especially the story of the Ormonds' house in Ciboure during the Second World War and its occupation by German troops. I have collected four other versions of this, besides my father's. Kitty Richardson has a brief account, and Chipps Bennett a fuller one in his memoirs; I have also included those of Derry and Julian Ormond. They all differ to some extent, although not radically (Cf. Appendix IV).

In the case of his mother's family, the Bishops, much of what he says was completely new to me. The most interesting discovery that I have made as a result is of the unpublished memoirs of Vyvien Hart-Davis, a younger sister of my grandmother, which are now in the Bodleian Library. These describe the time she spent with her husband, Charles, on the Gold Coast, Fiji, and Cyprus between 1908 and 1934, during his career as a colonial officer. I have included a shortened version of these in Appendix III.

For other parts of my father's life, there are various types of information, such as photographs, paintings, and letters. The most detailed records are of his time as an Autogiro pilot in the 1930s and his later career in the Army and with Westland, up to his retirement in 1962.

Two logbooks give precise records of his flying experience from 1932 to 1948, and there is also a large scrapbook of photos, letters, etc., from 1931 to 1962, together with various reports he wrote for the War Office on the development of the helicopter and its military value.

Some Personal Memories

I was born on 4 February 1940, but I have no memory of any events before my fourth birthday. By then, my parents were divorced. From 1944, I lived with my mother, and a series of nannies or housekeepers, in a cottage in Wiltshire (Manor Cottage, Hanging Langford, near Salisbury), until she died in December 1954, at the age of fifty-two.

There is a photograph on the occasion of my christening, which was at Lytchett Minster Church in Dorset, on 9 May 1940. This shows my uncle, Alex Allan, holding me, while my parents look on in an appreciative way, each with a glass of wine. There is no indication that anything unusual is happening in the world, apart from the fact that both my father and uncle are in military uniform. Yet the next day, Hitler's forces attacked Luxembourg, Belgium, and Holland, and Winston Churchill took over as prime minister (cf. Shakespeare, *Six Minutes in May* (2017), pp. 315–399). A few days later, both my father and uncle were fighting in France; within a couple of weeks, my uncle was taken prisoner, after the fall of Calais.

Where we lived for the next four years I do not know. My father seems to have been away for much of this time on his various military assignments. By 5 May 1944, at any rate, my parents were divorced, and he entered on a third marriage with Vivian Maitland, herself the divorced wife of Francis Pelham Maitland. In the 1930s, she had learnt to fly the Autogiro. This lasted officially until March 1952, although, in reality, it was probably a much shorter period. My father never mentioned this, except once. About this time, he married his last wife, Eleanor Ord McCrae.

When I was a boarder at West Downs in Winchester, between 1948 and 1953, my father used to come and take me out for the day sometimes. He liked to drive down to Hamble on the Solent and look at the boats there. For me, the main attraction of these trips was tea afterwards with fresh crab sandwiches. We also sometimes went down to the New Forest. He drove an old Singer *coupé*, nicknamed Gigli, after a famous tenor. On one occasion, he asked me if I had ever been driven at 90 mph. When I said 'no', he took us around the Winchester bypass at this speed. The car rattled and shook, but it held together. It was an exciting but also alarming experience, and on my return to school, it boosted my credit rating with my contemporaries. At this stage, however, he was still quite a stranger to me, and I was a bit scared of him.

When my mother died, I was in my second year as a scholar at Winchester. My father and uncle discussed what to do with me. I think that my uncle and aunt, who lived very near Winchester, offered to give me a home, but my father said that I should live with him and his wife, Eleanor, in Ashley Gardens in London. This was close to the office of Westland in the Sanctuary, where he then worked. I lived there until my second year at Oxford, and so we got to know one another rather better at this time.

Eleanor ('Aunt Lynn', as I learnt to call her) had worked for a number of the leading theatre and film directors and actors, such as Carol Reid and Laurence Olivier, so she had a lot of amusing stories about them. She was a talented musician and artist; she played the piano well. I was keen on the theatre as a teenager, with dreams of becoming an actor. I also started having piano lessons at school at the age of sixteen. We had lively parties at home with their friends, as well as evenings when my father's cousin, Clive Richardson, came for dinner with his wife, Aileen, and daughter, Angela. He was a well-known composer of light music, and there was a lot of happy piano-playing and singing. My father loved Spanish music and dancing; he used to strum his Spanish guitar.

He also used to take me to the air shows at Farnborough in the 1950s to see all the latest planes in action. Yet he never took me up in a helicopter. He used to say that they were 'dangerous brutes', since if the rotor failed, there was nothing to stop you from crashing, whereas the Autogiro was safer. He had lost two of his closest colleagues in an accident in 1950 when they were testing a new type of rotary-wing aircraft; he gave up flying as a pilot himself after that. Much later, we were on a normal passenger flight from Barcelona together, and I noticed that he seemed quite nervous and kept looking out of the window. He knew too much to feel secure. Ian Little, who was a rotary-wing aircraft test pilot during the Second World War, and had some very narrow escapes, also suffered later from a similar fear of flying.

At this time (late 1950s), I was aware that he was working on the plans for the new heliport at Battersea, but like most teenagers, I was living mostly in my own world, and so I took it all rather for granted. Once, I rashly asked him to explain how a car worked. He gave me a detailed technical explanation, which took at least an hour, but I have to confess that I forgot most of what he said soon afterwards.

Eleanor had survived a number of illnesses, such as tuberculosis, and operations when she was younger, and she was often unwell. My father worried a lot about her as a result. After he retired, they spent a lot of their time abroad, sometimes staying with friends in France and Jersey, but mainly renting a flat in Alicante on the Spanish east coast, for several months at a time, and letting their flat in London, which was by then in Embankment Gardens. I went out to stay with them occasionally for a week or two, and also saw something of them in London. He took up painting again, and we have some attractive oil paintings by him of scenes in Spain from this period.

When Jenny and I were married in 1968, my relationship with him and Eleanor became much better, as they got on so well with her. Two years later, they decided to sell their flat in London, settling at La Massana, in the mountains of Andorra. This was then a small village, but it has grown a lot with new development since then. Although my father did not ski any more, he loved the mountains and greatly enjoyed talking with those who did. I visited them and skied there, and they sometimes came and stayed with us. In the last two years of his life, when his health was failing, we drove down to Andorra with our children for summer holidays, staying in a hotel near them. He died on 25 March 1987, aged eighty-seven. Eleanor stayed in Andorra and died on 13 January 2000, aged ninety; she was born on 1 July 1909.

It has been an enjoyable task to edit these memoirs, especially listening to him telling stories that were sometimes familiar but quite often new, or which I had forgotten. One thread that seems to run through them all is my father's stubborn determination to go his own way. Since he was an only child of indulgent parents, any natural tendency of this kind seems to have been given free rein when he was small. When he walked out of his prep school because he was accused of something he had not done, his father took him skiing for the rest of the term. Unhappy at Harrow because his housemaster was only interested in good cricketers, he was removed by his mother after only four terms. As a young cavalry officer after the First World War, he decided to leave the Army and go out to South Africa, to try his hand as an orange farmer, because he thought it was too expensive to keep polo ponies out in Egypt, where they were due to be posted.

This independence helps to explain his decision in the early 1930s to learn how to fly the Autogiro, when it was still quite new, and then to get a commercial pilot's licence, something no one had ever done before with this type of machine. Not content with this, he also found time when working as a pilot to spend much of the winter in the Alps, helping to run various English ski clubs, and when in London to go to art school, following the example of his mother, who had been a professional artist, and two of her younger sisters.

When the next war came, he rejoined his old regiment, thanks to a meeting in the Alps with two of his brother officers, but the grim experience of fighting in France in a tank in 1940 convinced him that he could make better use of his flying knowledge in other ways, as an air liaison officer. Eventually, this led to his persuading the Army to send him to the States in order to learn how to fly the new Sikorsky helicopters, whose great military potential he already foresaw, although it took time and determination to convince the authorities of this.

Once retired, he was eager to get away from England, and his combined love of Spain and the mountains eventually took him and Eleanor to Andorra. Many of their fellow settlers had also led adventurous lives before, in places like Africa or sailing round the world in small boats, and had no wish to return to England. A good case would be their close friends, Edward and Clare Allcard. Edward (who died in 2017 at the age of 102) was the first yachtsman to sail across the Atlantic single-handed in both directions. His later sailing adventures with Clare are described in her book *A Gypsy Life* (2016). Even before this, in London, they had some unusual acquaintances—for example, Kim Philby, whom they found an amusing dinner companion, never suspecting what he was really up to. Something about his raffish cosmopolitanism must have struck a chord with my father, especially after a few drinks.

What may not be so obvious is the degree of insecurity, financial as well as physical, involved in some of these adventures, especially in the 1930s, when jobs were hard to find. The life of an Autogiro pilot was precarious and probably not well paid. One can get a sense of this from letters to my mother in 1936, shortly before his boss, Juan de la Cierva, was killed in a civil aircraft accident. My father believed, rightly or wrongly, that this was due to sabotage because of Cierva's close involvement with Franco at the time. His first marriage had broken down, and when he and my mother married in December 1936, the prospect of another war was very real. Escaping to the Alps that winter, they were not destined to enjoy a settled life for long before war broke out. My mother was not well, and he was then constantly on the move. It was not perhaps really until he was in his fifties that he began to live a more settled life.

It is tempting to see this as a pattern that occurred with other adventurous characters of this period. A famous example would be Paddy Leigh Fermor. His extraordinary war career and also his gift for words set him apart, but one can see the same bloody-minded refusal to toe the line. My father was a good raconteur, but he was often rather modest about what he had done. It seems typical that when the heliport at Battersea was opened, an achievement due very much to his initiative, his boss at Westland, Eric Mensforth, was rewarded with a knighthood, whereas (as he says, without further comment) he himself was given in gratitude a silver cigarette box.

The Autogiro and the Early Development of the Helicopter

The name 'Autogiro' (with capital 'A') was the spelling patented by Juan de la Cierva, to describe a rotary-wing aircraft of the type he designed. Rotary-wing planes in general are also known as gyroplanes or autogyros.

The first Autogiro models were tested in 1922, and the first to make a successful flight of about 200 yards was in January 1923. Autogiros were equipped with a propeller, as well as a rotor. The basic point about the rotor was that it rotated freely—without being powered. By contrast, helicopters have a powered rotor and no propeller at the front. The early types of Autogiro were started either by taxiing round the airfield until the rotor was spinning (which was unsatisfactory) or by pulling a cord wrapped around the hub. In later models, the rotor was started by the engine. Once the rotor speed was sufficient, the clutch was disengaged and it then spun freely.

A major advance came in 1932 with the development of 'direct control'. This meant that all movement could be directed by tilting the rotor blades fore and aft or sideways. The most successful type made by Cierva using this technique was the C.30, developed from 1933 onwards. The other important factor in the successful Autogiros was that the rotor blades were not rigid but able to move up and down. The blades thus automatically adjusted to the differences

Rotor head of Autogiro (from scrapbook). Photograph by Curtis Moffat, Kathleen Allan's husband. Reproduced also in Barnes, *Curtis Moffat: Silver Society* (2016), no. 145.

of airflow speed, avoiding any tendency to roll. A further development was the C.40, or 'jump take-off' model, available from 1938 onwards.

The chief advantages of the Autogiro were that they were reasonably safe, especially as they could be landed at low speed; simple to control; and could take off and land in a very small area. They were in fact both safer than the helicopter and also quieter.

During the Second World War, Autogiros in Britain were used for observation work, but especially for radar calibration, in connection with the new radar stations. Although they could not hover, they were able to fly in very tight circles over a particular spot and so make more accurate observations than other aircraft.

The first practical helicopters date from 1935–6, and it is claimed that the first flight was made in France by Maurice Claise on 26 June 1935, with a double-rotor model (although my father doubts whether this was a true helicopter; cf. chapter 13). After Cierva's death in 1936, those in charge of his company in Britain turned their attention more towards helicopter development, although work on the Autogiro continued in the United States up to the Second World War, led by Harold Pitcairn and Wallace Kellett; Cierva had assigned all his patents to Pitcairn. Yet the Autogiro was less suitable for long-distance flying, and from 1939, Igor Sikorsky began designing single-rotor helicopters in the States. The first free flight with one of these was made on 13 May 1940. From 1942, production began on a better version of this (VS-316 or R-4).

In Britain, the authorities failed to support local development of the helicopter during the War, preferring to rely on America for this. Hence the first helicopters were ordered from the States. After the War ended, however, Westland made a series of agreements with Sikorsky and were able to take over US technology, using their own finance. They soon got a clear lead over other British firms, which were relying on inadequate government support. As a result, by 1960, they had acquired the monopoly of helicopter development in Britain.

An excellent account of the C.30 Autogiro is given by one its leading pilots, Reginald Brie, in *The Autogiro and how to Fly it* (second edition, 1935). On the history of rotorcraft, including both gyroplanes and helicopters, see Brie, *A History of British Rotorcraft 1866–1965* (1968); Brooks, *Cierva Autogiros: The Development of Rotary-Wing Flight* (1988); and Uttley, *Westland and the British Helicopter Industry 1945–60* (2013). On the life of Juan de la Cierva, see also Ord-Hume, *Juan de la Cierva and his Autogiros* (2011). See also the recorded interview with Brie about his career, referred to in chapter 10, note 4 below. The voice of Igor Sikorsky can be heard in the recording of the lecture he gave in 1967 on acceptance of the Wright Brothers Memorial Trophy: soundcloud.com/aerosociety-podcast/sets/classic-lecture-series. In addition, the National Aerospace Library at Farnborough has two collections of photographs relating to the history of early rotorcraft, that of Alan Marsh (donated by his son, Neil) and Basil Arkell (donated by his son, John).

1

Family and Early Years

I was born on 8 October 1899 at 28 Roland Gardens, Kensington, London. It was a narrow and old-fashioned house—six floors and a basement. No lift, of course. My nursery was on the fourth floor. The servants lived up above me.[1]

My earliest recollections are of London streets, being taken to the Park from Roland Gardens. My earliest memory of all is of a beggar, who sat at the corner of Gloucester Road. He smelt considerably, and that is how I remember him. My dog, Sam, is my other early recollection. He was a spaniel and he smelt too, rather similarly to the beggar.

Not long after I was born, we acquired a cottage in Surrey, called Emley, not very far from Godalming.[2] That was the local railway station. It was a very nice old cottage, going back to Elizabethan times. It was part of a farm, the farmyard being on the other side of the road, and the farmer having a separate house of later vintage. It was not very habitable, as it had an enormous tank for rainwater in the middle, our only source of supply, and that made the whole house most abominably damp. Yet we never used it except in summer. My father, who was an ardent horticulturalist, spent quite a lot of time in the garden there. Yet his principal amusement, and indeed work, was at the John Innes Horticultural Institution outside London, where he worked under Bateson, a very celebrated professor of genetics, in fact more or less the inventor of genetics.[3]

We usually went to Switzerland, my father being very keen on skiing, which he had learnt to play at when he was in Norway. He had gone to Norway originally to fish salmon. He got on very well with the Norwegians, and they invited him to stay over in the winter, and see what their other sport was like. He did that with my uncle Teddy, and they became quite reasonably expert skiers for that day, also doing a bit of jumping.[4] They then decided to ski nearer home, and so they went to Davos, in due course founding the Davos English Ski Club, which was the parent of the Ski Club of Great Britain, and one of the first ski clubs in Europe.[5]

Mabel with Jack in 1899.

Jack Richardson as a baby.

Above left: Charles William Richardson, Jack's father, at Holmenkollen in Norway, where he and his brother Teddy first learnt to ski in 1894–5. The date on this photograph is wrong.

Above right: Edward Cleland Richardson skiing. (*British Ski Year Book for 1954*, p. 161)

Skiing entered my life when I was a tiny boy. My father used to take me out. He used to tow me behind him or carry me in a rucksack. I learnt to ski when I was very small, and that knowledge stayed with me. That is the time when you should learn a game like that. My father was very kind and very patient.

My mother did not like Switzerland and, unfortunately, suffered very severely from rheumatism. In those days, doctors did not understand that exercise is good for rheumatism. She was told to lie up in easy chairs, long chairs on balconies, and in the sun. She tried that in Davos and got very bored with it, and so she took to going to the South of France. Eventually, my father would take us down to a villa or hotel in Cannes and install us there, then go off skiing for a month or two, and come back round about Easter time perhaps.

We spent quite a lot of time in France and lived for a while in Paris when I was a very small child. I do not remember much about that, excepting the home of my cousins, David Richardson's family. Uncle David was the senior of my father's family, and he had a family of five—two boys and three girls. They were my closest relations—in fact, the only ones I ever saw anything of at that time. I was a little scared of them. Some were older than me. Barney was a year younger. Bruce was about three or four years older. Nancy came after Bruce, then there was Kitty, who was a shade younger than me, and Nonie, who was in those days a baby. They lived in Paris when they were not in Brittany, and we saw quite a lot of them when they were there. They spent most of their summers in Brittany. Later, they moved from Brittany to St Jean de Luz, where my uncle built a house, which is still in use, but not by the family.[6]

So I spent quite a lot of my early childhood in France and naturally picked up a way of talking French, which unfortunately was the servants' way. At my prep school later, the lady who taught us French, who was unfortunately the sister of the headmaster, did not understand what I was talking about half the time. Yet when she did, she was extremely scandalised because the expressions I was using were often very far from polite. I suffered a little bit for that. However, the ability to use colloquial French, the French of the streets so to speak, was very useful to me later on in life, especially when motoring in Paris. Driving a car through Paris, it is very useful to be able to answer back.

My father was a strong man. He could carry my mother upstairs from the basement to the top floor, and Mummy was not a small woman. He often did this trick after dinner. My father was a Scot, on both sides. My grandfather married twice. His first wife died, and my father was of the second family.[7] My grandfather was a 'sugar man'. We owned land in Mauritius and brought the sugar cane to Scotland in our own ships. The family were all good sailors and fine yachtsmen, but curiously enough, we seem never to have had any member of it in the Navy. My grandfather owned the largest yacht on the Clyde, the *Selene*. She was the twin sister of the *Britannia*, the King's cutter. I believe that

David Bruce Richardson, second son of David Richardson of Hartfield, drawn by Percival Tudor-Hart.

David Bruce with his wife, Margaret, and his sister, Nelly (Agnes Ellen).

my grandfather held records for passages between Scotland and Portugal.[8] My grandfather owned the first steam launch on the Clyde (or so I have been told), and if he could not get up the Clyde and into his office, in Glasgow, then nothing could get there by water. That was his reputation.[9]

My grandparents lived at Hartfield, a very large and very ugly house overlooking the Clyde.[10] All the boys sailed. My father could certainly go down the Clyde and around the west coast when he was sixteen. He and Teddy would sail together.

My grandfather died in 1896. The sugar business had not prospered during his later years, owing to the arrival of German beet sugar, which could undercut the cane, since it cost little to import. The Lyle family, our rivals, were cleverer than we were and invented golden syrup, which kept them going. My grandfather was not so bright. So, after my grandfather's death, the eldest son, David, sold the business. There was enough to provide everyone with a reasonable income, for that day. So why go on working?

My father was intended for the Kirk, a minister to see to the family soul. Yet he had studied comparative religion when at Cambridge and had to admit to his parent that he could not be sure as to which religion he could practice, 'maybe Buddhism'! So his father told him to read law in the future because he seemed to have the gift of the gab. My father did so and duly 'ate his dinners'. Yet he was never called to the Bar; I think this was because my grandfather's death left him with what then seemed to be enough (about £2–3,000 a year). So why take the bread out of some less fortunate mouth? That attitude was quite well understood in the days of good King Edward VII.

Yet my mother (Mabel) had very expensive tastes. She liked clothes; she liked new clothes particularly because, coming in the middle of a large family, she had never had any of her own. My mother came from a large family of thirteen children.[11] The family name was Bishop. There were still a number of country cousins, owning large properties. The only one I ever came across was known as Duke Bishop. He was a cousin of my mother's and had a very extensive farm somewhere in the Chilterns. I remember a very big farmhouse, a beautiful house with a lot of land. He was what was known as a gentleman farmer. He spent a great deal of his time hunting and shooting, and his farm was, I presume, run largely by tenants.[12]

My grandfather (Edgar) had been pretty well off.[13] Edgar and his brother, Henry, were directors of Gunter's. This was one of the leading eating-places in London, a place where you got wonderful cakes, and they made all the wedding cakes for every wedding of any consequence. His wife was Sarah Kimberley.[14] I do not know very much about her. She looked exactly like old Queen Victoria, but then all old ladies looked like Queen Victoria in that day and age. She was completely and absolutely scatty, and was simply being looked after.

Mabel Bishop, Jack's mother, in 1898.

Charles William Richardson.

Charles Bishop, with his two sons, Edgar (Jack's maternal grandfather) and Henry. Cf. Appendix II.

Henry Bishop hunting, a drawing by his son Harry.

My maternal grandfather was a country gent. He was a bit of a fast liver. He liked to drive his carriage behind his pair, or four, or tandem, wearing a large buttonhole at horse shows. I believe he did very well at that, but it was a very expensive hobby, and it got through certainly his own fortune and a considerable amount of his wife's. He came to London in middle life, and the family occupied a very large rather barrack-like house north of the Park.[15]

My mother had nine sisters and three brothers. My uncle Harry was a soldier in the Lancashire Fusiliers, and later commanded their First Battalion. Uncle Harry was my mother's favourite brother. He married Olive Sylvester, a very beautiful woman.[16]

Their daughter, Molly Bishop, eventually became an artist like my mother, but even better than my mother.[17] She got a job as a caricaturist for the *Bystander*. This meant that no party of any importance in London could happen without my cousin Molly's attendance, to make at least one full page of caricatures. Without that, the party did not exist. The result of this was that Molly became very much a socialite and later married extremely well, her husband, Lord George Scott, being a close relative of the Royal Family and having a considerable title.[18] Funnily enough, he was an officer in one of the other regiments that formed part of our brigade in France.[19] I did not know my cousin, Molly, very well. When she was a little girl, she was brought to see us. She was very small, and she was set down in the centre of our drawing room. Molly was very beautiful, and also an extremely good painter, and very well qualified indeed, quite apart from her caricatures. After she married, of course, she ceased that kind of work, but she continued to paint up to probably quite late in life; a good deal of her work was exhibited. Her portraits were good and altogether I think she was a very talented person. I liked Molly. We only came up against each other latterly, when the war started, when her husband and I were brigaded together at Tidworth, and might have seen a little more of each other than we did. In any case, we were all far too busy learning to handle our tanks and we did not have very much time for social activity just then.

There was also my Uncle Darell, who had gone out to South Africa as a doctor during the South African War and remained out there.[20] It eventually transpired that he had married a woman of French extraction. There are in South Africa a great many formerly French people, whose history goes back to the Huguenot time, when they escaped from France and joined the Dutch out there. The mixture of Dutch and French is an extremely good and very charming one, and I think the nicest people in South Africa are of that persuasion. When my mother went out to South Africa, she went in search of him and found him on a diamond field recently opened, doing extremely well as a doctor and married to this very charming lady. I think she was rather a disappointment to my mother.

Above left: Colonel H. O. (Harry) Bishop, 1st Battalion Lancashire Fusiliers. He was in command at Gallipoli during the 'Lancashire landing', when six VCs were won before breakfast.

Above right: *Harry Bishop*, a drawing by his daughter, Molly.

Below: 'Molly and her Daddy going for a drive to the sea, Karachi, with love to Uncle Bill and cousin Jack.'

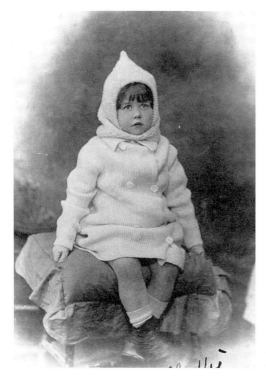

Molly Bishop in 1914, aged two
or three.

Harry Oswald Mannin ('Tim')
Bishop, Molly's brother.

There was another uncle, Hugh, who went out to Africa. Tragically, he died out there.[21]

Mother, when she was seventeen or eighteen, went to the Slade Art School. There, she studied under Henry Tonks, who became a great friend of the Bishop family.[22] Tonks had a good deal of time for Mama. So, when she got married, he said to her, 'My dear, I can't possibly afford to give you a wedding present, but I'll paint your first-born'. So, when I was born, I was painted by Tonks, a wet but very well-painted baby.[23]

Our house in Kensington was frequented by a mixed lot of artists, one or two poets, people of an artistic description, and my mother's family, or rather the females of it, since three of her sisters met their forthcoming husbands in our drawing room. Mama seems to have got on very well with the rest of her family in those days, but, for reasons unknown to me, the family feeling broke up later on. I do not think it was my fault, though I was not a very nice little boy. As an only child (Mama firmly refused to have any more), I was hideously spoilt. My father was very kind; I loved him. Mama would give me anything to keep me quiet. I very soon discovered my way about, so to speak, and did not learn any new tricks until very much later, when I went to Sandhurst.

Mother was good, particularly at sculptured work. After leaving the Slade, she worked for some six or seven years as an artist. She horrified the family by sharing a studio with a man. I think it was all perfectly moral, and Mother lived at home. For some years, she operated from that studio and other places, painting and sculpting. She did much decoration (including, I believe, two ships) and portraits. Her work was fresh and good. Later, when my parents lived in Paris, she had two paintings and some portrait busts accepted for the Salon d'Automne, in 1904, and her paintings were displayed among the men's works, which was unusual for a woman at that date.[24]

She continued to paint portraits and to do a certain amount of clay work after her marriage, but it gradually died out. She almost gave up painting altogether, but she did fortunately continue caricature for quite a long time, and there are a few drawings of hers left. Later Mama lived very largely in France. She loved the French and France, and living in smallish hotels, with little communities of their own of foreigners to France, she made many friends. She made many caricatures of her friends, but she usually gave them away, so we do not have them. I am very sorry because my mother was a good caricaturist.

When we went out to South Africa, my mother very speedily persuaded my father to take her out there. On arrival, she found that the hotels were not places for lying up. You would be invaded by rather smelly houseboys at a fairly early hour in the day. If you were in bed, so much the worse. So you got up, and the fact of having to get up not only saved, but very nearly cured my mother. After she had been in South Africa for a couple of years,

Mabel sketching.

Copy of bust of Jack by Mabel
Richardson, exhibited at the Salon d'
Automne, Paris, in 1904.

Lady in feathered hat, a drawing by
Mabel Richardson.

Lady Brougham and Vaux, a photograph (1906).

Lady Brougham and Vaux, a
drawing by Mabel Richardson.

'*Désirée*'. Copy of bust
by Mabel Richardson,
exhibited at the Salon
d'Automne, Paris, in 1904.

Mabel in 1918.

she had very little more rheumatism. This was partly due to the climate, but it was very largely because she had to get up and to get out. She had to take a certain amount of exercise, all of which was extremely good for her. When she came back from South Africa, she was really almost cured of her rheumatism, and from that time on until almost the start of the Second World War, she lived very largely in France. Mummy and Daddy never got on at all after I was about seven or eight years old. I remember the most horrible quarrels happening between them. I am afraid that I was the kind of small boy who took advantage of the quarrels. I was able to get one or other on my side. It did not matter which it was, but if I could not get my way from one, I could get my way from the other one. That of course was extremely bad for me.

Two of Mother's younger sisters followed her to the Slade, Constance (Connie) and Vyvien. They were twins, born in 1884. Together with Gladys, who was born in 1882, they were known as the three Graces or the three Bishop beauties. They really were extremely beautiful girls and fitted the rather statuesque appearance of the day, with big busts.[25]

So far as I know, Connie and Vyvien did not work at any form of art after leaving the Slade. I do not know what happened to Connie after her return from Russia, just before 1914; she had been governess there in a sparklingly aristocratic family, very close to the Tsar.[26] I do not think she ever married. Gladys married a chap with large interests in Rhodesia, which was a very young place in those days.[27] I believe that, before her death, she was one of the best-off women in Rhodesia. I knew two of their children from time to time, since they were in England during the war, and I saw a bit of them then. Vyvien married Charlie Hart-Davis, who was a wealthy young man with a very large background.[28] They rather faded out of my mother's existence, or shall we say that my mother and father faded out of theirs? I think the trouble was that my parents could not keep up with them, and my mother was rather jealous.

We used to have a very pretty, fan-shaped painting, of a size to fit above a doorway. It was really a beautiful painting, of the three sisters. I do not know who painted it (Tonks?) or what became of it.[29]

There was another aunt who looked after me for some time as a sort of subsidiary nanny, my Aunt Sydney.[30] She married somebody in Canadian Pacific and disappeared into Canada for ever. She was very much my favourite aunt, I think, simply because she nannied me for some time. My original nanny was a country girl from Surrey. She came out to France with us a couple of times, and then she married a local policeman. She was a nice girl and looked after me extremely well. Aunt Sydney was a kind of stopgap, who used to come and look after me when my proper nanny was on holiday.

Another auntie of mine, my aunt Dolly, was married to a chap called Tip Richards, who was partly American.[31] Tip's family was very well off, and his mother owned Steephill Castle in the Isle of Wight. Steephill Castle was a

Above: Connie, Vyvien, and Gladys Bishop, younger sisters of Mabel, known as 'the three Bishop beauties'.

Left: Connie Bishop.

Vyvien Bishop.

Gladys Bishop.

Charles Hart-Davis, Vyvien Bishop's husband.

Charles Hart-Davis as district commissioner for Nicosia in Cyprus (1922–34). Charles is greeting the governor general of Cyprus and his wife.

large rambling place, with a railway line running through the grounds. We used to go and stay at the resort of St Lawrence, a small place on a very steep hill not far from the castle. The house we took was owned by a writer, of quite considerable Edwardian notoriety I believe, a woman.[32]

My aunt at Steephill was a curious person. She played the large organ in the Castle. Whenever I went there, I used to be paraded beside the organ and made to sing a hymn, which I hated. I had two cousins there, Arnold and Jimmie. One of them was my age and the other was a little older. They bullied me most unmercifully. The great idea was to play Red Indians in the grounds. I was the 'white sacrifice' always, usually pinned up against a tree. They terrified me. What happened to them later in life, I do not know. Yet Steephill Castle and visits to it were rather alarming as a result both of the cousins and of the organ.

My uncle—Selby Ormond, who had eloped with my father's favourite sister, Nelly—was in the Lancashire Fusiliers. His best friend was my mother's brother, Harry, just a bit younger, but in the same regiment. Each in turn commanded the First Battalion during the First World War at Gallipoli, that great mistake made by Winston Churchill—Uncle Selby before the landing, and Uncle Harry during and after the landing. Both survived that war.[33] Selby then settled at Ciboure, the fishing port of St Jean de Luz.[34] Yet the uncles would never acknowledge each other's existence. Uncle Selby had eloped with Nelly, who climbed out of the bathroom window to go to him, so the story was always told. My uncle David was sent, by Papa, to make sure that they got properly married. Selby could never forgive that insult. So, the two families could often be seen at tables in the Casino restaurant (the meeting place of St Jean). The younger members would dance together, but their elders never saw one another. Thus it continued until death ended the story. My aunts' curiosity about each other's household was insatiable. So, if you went to stay at one house, you would always be invited to the other.

The Basques are a curious race. My cousin, Pat Ormond, made a study of them over many years.[35] No one knows where they came from or when. Yet they are loyal to their friends. During 1939–45, my uncle Selby's house was occupied by the Germans. A brigadier lived there for some time. That house had two entrances. It was on a very steep hillside, with one entrance two floors above the other. Before Uncle bought it, the house had been used by smugglers. While the brigadier was there, many of our escaping prisoners of war were passed through the upper part. After the war, the senior local fish-wife of Ciboure and the former leading *contrebandiers* were invited to Buckingham Palace and decorated. Ciboure is very proud of that. If the Germans admired any piece of furniture, it would at once disappear 'for repairs'. I was staying in the house when some of it came back from the mountains on muleback.[36]

Bust of Selby Ormond, the husband of Nelly, by Mabel Richardson.

Nelly (Agnes Ellen) Ormond, sister of Charles William Richardson.

Pat and Kitty Ormond, the children of Selby and Nelly.

2

Prep Schools

I was sent to a boarding school when I was about seven. I do not consider that to be necessarily too young to send a kid to school, but it is rather young to send one to a boarding school when they had never been away from home before and did not understand living with other children. My first experience there was shattering. Somebody kicked a football at me, and I did not know what it was. Naturally, I became a 'guy' at once. I knew little of other children and I had played none of their games. So, I was very lonely, very frightened, and most unhappy. It was a rough school, and I was taken away after a year.

I do not know whether that was a good or a bad thing, but my second prep school was smaller, considerably more comfortable, and considerably nicer.[1] There was no bullying, whereas at the first one, I was bullied all the time. I was not unhappy there, but when I was about eleven, I was accused, quite wrongly, of having done something very naughty, which I had not done. The powers that were said that I ought to be punished because I would not own up. The headmaster was in a bad temper and refused to believe me. I was very upset by this, as I thought it most unfair, so I took my school cap off my head and walked out of the place the very next afternoon. I went into Ramsgate, which must have been 7 or 8 miles away. I spent the afternoon at Ramsgate. I only spent a few pence on a glass of lemonade. In the evening, I took a train to London. I remember it cost 6s/8d and I just had enough in my pocket. There were very cheap fares in those days from places of that kind. Ramsgate, Margate, and so on were holiday places for east London, and as east London was the cheaper end of London, so these places also were inexpensive to get to, especially at the weekend. I arrived at Kings Cross long after midnight and walked to our flat in Kensington. I had to ask the way frequently of policemen. My family had already been told that I was missing and had warned the London police, but no one stopped me. They merely patted me on the head. I got back to our flat at about 1 a.m. to a rather upset family. I was kissed, petted, and put to bed.

The next day, what to do? My father decided not send me back that term, which was probably a wise decision. It was getting quite late in the term. Daddy leapt at the chance of going skiing early, and he took me out on his own to Samedan, near St Moritz; he really taught me for the first time the beginnings of skiing. That winter was when I really learnt the art of the game. What I learnt was to stand up. I think this winter probably had a considerable effect on my later life from a sports point of view. When I got back to school, I had become a popular hero, so my life there became very happy for my last year.

Skiing is a funny job. When I came back from Africa in 1929, I had almost forgotten how to ski. I had not skied at all since 1914. That is a very long time. Yet when I put the damn boards on, I found somehow that they fitted into my feet, and my feet somehow fitted into the boards, and there was no problem. One fell, of course, but anyone learning to ski falls. Falling is something that you avoid only later, because the later it is in your life, the more likely you are to get an injury. So, it is advisable that you learn not to fall. I suppose it was inevitable that I should go back to the mountains. South Africa had nothing of that sort to offer, and in any case, I could not have taken the offer—I was far too busy with my farm.

Jack on skis, around 1908.

3

Harrow and Gabby's Crammer

I went to Harrow about a year before the First World War started. Yet the house I went to was not a good one. It was run by a housemaster who was more interested in cricket than anything else in the world. So, everyone had to play cricket, or they did not matter. Generally, the place was full of bullying and not at all a kind sort of place for a small boy from a rather private prep school. I was no good at cricket, so got on very badly all round, so I hated Harrow.[1]

Soon after the war began, I was removed from Harrow and sent to an army 'crammer'.[2] My father was working in London, and my mother managed to have me removed from school. Gabbitas, who ran the crammer, was a shocking old fraud. My father wanted me to go to Woolwich, to become a gunner or a sapper. For the Woolwich entrance exam, chemistry was essential. Gabby had no one to teach chemistry. There were glass jars and retorts in evidence in the hall, but they were never used. The old rascal did not tell my father. He told me, however, that I was already quite advanced enough to pass into Sandhurst. I need only keep up to that level and I would pass in easily. So why worry? I was already well aware that the expectation of life after leaving Sandhurst (or Woolwich) was six months; that fact of life we all of us knew and endeavoured to forget. The war could go on for ever. So, what? I did very little work at Gabby's.

Mrs Gabby was a plump lady, who had been on the stage (on the boards as they called it in those days), I think in the chorus in very second-rate shows. She was kind-hearted and liked to take some of us seventeen-year olds to the theatre, partly to introduce us to 'les girls'. Afterwards, we might dine with some of the chorus. It was all very harmless and quite good for us, all quite moral and rather good fun. All we did was go to some restaurant and have a slap-up meal together. Yet, in a way, I suppose it was a little bit upsetting for some of the boys. It did not worry me. The meals were paid for by Gabby, who

Jack at Harrow.

put them on our bill. I learnt to fish at Gabby's. There were several large carp ponds nearby, some of them dating back to the days of the Romans, and also an excellent trout stream not very far off. Gabby made no difficulty about my spending an entire day if I wanted out fishing. I took a book with me, or some papers to read up, and might even possibly do a little work.

In the winter, I was able to get away and do a bit of hunting. This sport, in fact, had come my way a year or so before I went to Gabby's. I met a woman (Barbara Goring), an Australian, who lived with an older sister near Battle Abbey, who had horses. She was my first girlfriend. Barbara and I were sexless sweethearts. She was a good deal older than I was. The link was the horse, the horse, and nothing but the horse. She was a very ardent horse girl, and she taught me most of what I learnt about riding in those days. Then she took me out cubbing. When I finally started hunting properly, I think I fell over nearly every gate in East Sussex, but I loved it. It was fun and it was very inexpensive. In fact, it very often cost me next to nothing at all, for the simple reason that my riding was good enough for exercising the horse and the local job stables were very anxious to have their horses exercised. I was ready to do it for them. I learnt probably a good deal more than I thought I did. That was supplemented by some stays down in Exmoor, rushing after the stag down there. I had an old, a very old motorbike, on which to get across the country. Later, Barbara married a naval officer, after the war.

Barbara Gorton, Jack's first girl-friend and riding companion.

4
Sandhurst (1917–8)

I was a year at Sandhurst, from age seventeen and a half. I liked the place, partly because the discipline, which was very harsh, being based on that of the Guards regiments, suited me. You had very little time off, but as long as you did what you were told, you could be reasonably happy. The discipline protected one, in a way, but also, I was quite a popular cadet. My company (there were twelve) was 'champion company'. I rode for the company, and we did rather well. By the time I got to Sandhurst, I could ride reasonably well. That was why I went into a cavalry regiment, to which three of my friends were going, all being sons of country gentry. One was told, too, that cavalry officers could get into the Flying Corps—newly formed, glamorous, and far more comfortable than a trench. Cavalry were supposed to have 'hands', and also, they had been trained as scouts. Scouting was the main job of the Flying Corps at that time.

At Sandhurst, one was not forced to play particular games. I played tennis (very badly) and golf (also badly). Golf was fun because it meant you could get away from the place, and sometimes, my father could come and play with me; those were red-letter days. In winter, I went running after beagles, which was probably much better for me than football, as I was extremely bad at all ball games. I was never good at hitting anything with a bat, a racket, my feet, or (for that matter) a shotgun. Yet I was an excellent rifle shot because you could dwell on your aim as long as you liked. I boxed but did not care for it, and so I never took it seriously. In riding, we did not get the saddle, the award for the best riders, but my friend Ronnie Macdonell did. We won the company jumping competition. We were champions two terms out of the three I was there.

We had one of the King's sons, Prince Henry, in our company. I did not see much of him; he was junior to me.[1] He was a pleasant fellow but with not much to say for himself. Yet there was one occasion when he had been over to

Above: The Royal Military College, Sandhurst (1917), 'H' Company. Jack is second from left in the back row.

Left: Jack in uniform (1918).

Windsor, or what he called Windsor, on what was called 10.45 leave, which meant you had to be back by 10.45 p.m. That sounds easy enough, but it meant leaving London not later than 8 p.m. by tube from Piccadilly. If you did that and your bicycle was at Hounslow, you might just make it. Unfortunately, I had just on this occasion not made it. So, the following morning, I was up before the company commander. I was jolly glad to see that Prince Henry was up too. I thought that, at any rate, would mitigate matters. Not at all. We both got the maximum amount of pack drill that could be served to a cadet—a month on the square—which meant every spare available hour, you had to get into your army pack, full pack, and be drilled by one of the sergeant majors. It was very far from pleasant.

5

Ireland (1918)

I had passed my entrance exam very well (thanks to Gabby's notes), and I passed out very near the top of the list. I was commissioned in August 1918. I was sent to the Light Cavalry Depot at the Curragh Camp in County Kildare, not far from Dublin. My regiment was the Ninth Lancers. One should remember that Ireland was all still then a part of the British Isles. So, Ireland had been at war with Germany, not neutral, as was the south in the Second World War.

I was still there when we were told that the war was over, on 11 November, expecting at any moment to be sent to France. We were told that we could disappear for the day. I had won a motorcycle the night before at some game (my first and practically my only win at cards; we used to play cards at the Curragh pretty regularly, and most of the night) off a chap who could not pay me in money. It was a very old one. I did not ride a motorbike very well, but I took it, and I set forth for Dublin next day on it. I could not get there because some road-mender had heard that there was an armistice and left his tools dumped in the middle of the road, just around the corner. I hit them. That rather spoilt my day for me, but I did get to Dublin eventually, and I seem to remember a riotous party happening at Jamie's Restaurant.

Jamie's Restaurant was the centre of Dublin in those days, not only for the horse people (it was one of the betting centres); it was also very much patronised by the stage and by the intellectuals. It served the most excellent food. It was a remarkable place. It certainly went on for a very long time. I last went there about the middle of 1942, and it had not changed at all. The food was just as good, and the lights were full on since Dublin was in a neutral state. The interesting thing about Jamie's was that in the Second World War, you could even meet your German counterpart there, and a story, which I firmly believe to be true, is told about a certain naval commander who was hunting a submarine. They used to take refuge in Southern Ireland waters in the harbours there, which was perfectly safe. The naval man used to lie up outside waiting for it. One day, the submarine had been talking to its home on the radio, and the British commander got the callsign and was able to chip in. The net result of that was that they organised a meeting for dinner at Jamie's in Dublin. I am one of those who firmly believe that that dinner happened. Anyway, Dublin was a very nice place during the Second World War, when all the lights were on and all the shops were open.

The Curragh was fun. It was run entirely by wounded or sick officers, who had been out at the front and invalided home. Their ideas were pretty wide, and it was an easy place to get away from on leave, provided your leave was in Ireland. There was a good deal of Sinn Fein activity at the time, but it did not affect us at the Curragh, an entirely military camp. Later, it certainly did.

I had two girlfriends, each a Barbara. The second one was far more feminine than the first. She was a very pretty little doll, who could dance well and sing like an angel. She took music and singing very, very seriously, studying hard under a fierce music master. She had a very good, very sweet voice. Her papa was an ex-tea man, having a large house in Hampstead. Papa did not quite approve of me, and I was far too young anyway, so he sent B. B. as she was called to China, to an uncle's house in Shanghai. B. B. liked the voyage out; she had almost forgotten me by the time the ship sailed, so I guess, but there was a most attractive ship's 'bad man' aboard—there always was; they played cards well—so B. B. fell for that, which caused a lot of trouble in Shanghai, where he lived.

Well, these were my first and so very properly moral loves. Then I met Delia, and that was very different. I had left the regiment in 1921. At about that time, I met Delia and immediately decided that I must marry her. She was of the same opinion. It lasted fourteen years, but we began to split after the traditional seven, when we returned from Africa.

6
Germany (1918–9)

I eventually joined the regiment sometime around the end of November 1918, when it was just over the frontier of Germany.[1] Not long after, we moved further in, and as the escort to the divisional general, were accommodated in a very fine old *Schloss*, in which we had our mess, with our horses and men in an aluminium factory about half a mile away. It was a beautiful place, rather forbidding, and very ghostly.[2] About Christmas time, when you went to see to the men and horses as orderly officer of the day, you had to walk that half-mile alone at night, in snow, along an avenue of tall trees. The trees did not feel friendly. The shadows were horrid. On the way back to the *Schloss*, it was always worse. There were two unfriendly gates and two moats to cross, as well as the outer courtyard, where things seemed to lurk.

It was inhabited almost entirely by women. Old ladies appeared apparently from nowhere at all. Doors were concealed in the passage walls. The owner had a son who had been captured by the British, and he had heard that his son was being well-treated in his prison camp. So, the old count was extremely nice to us. However, the majordomo did not like us at all, and he arranged that our officer's mess room, the one we retired to after dinner, should be the haunted chamber of the castle. Nothing appeared, but you just could not stay in that room after midnight. That is a fact; no one could. We never learnt just precisely what it was, but it was certainly something pretty nasty. When we enquired about it, we got laughed at. That was where the majordomo got his own back. We were rather a wild crowd. There was an Australian subaltern who was an expert with a stock-whip. He could knock a fly off a man's back without hurting him. Unfortunately, he had a row with the majordomo and chased him round the courtyard with his whip. He cracked his whip all round him but never touched him. The majordomo never forgave him, and it was after this that we were moved to the haunted room.

In spring 1919, we moved into Cologne and were housed on the banks of the Rhine, at the Exhibition Ground. Cologne was a lovely place. We were close to the cathedral, near the Cathedral Bridge. We had a box in the opera house, which did not appeal much to the cavalry taste, but I used to occupy it when I could. I listened to most of Wagner's *Ring* there, as well as other German operas. The Opera House was strange, particularly during the intervals, when everybody was outside on the steps. You saw every kind of Allied uniform, some of the smartest being the Italian cavalry in their cloaks. We had Americans there, too, and that caused our poor subalterns a certain amount of grief, as our riding master, the most important man in our lives at that time, decided that we were going to ride better than the Americans. They had formed a tented circus, and they drove it through Cologne and gave displays outside. Anything the Americans could do in their circus, we had to perform in our riding school. It was painful, for example, when you were learning to straddle three horses, and they opened out so that you came down very painfully on the centre one. Yet it was fun. We learnt to ride bareback, to jump on to a horse's back, and to stand there when it was at a gallop. A lot of tricks we learnt, and then we finally staged our own circus, much to the amusement of the Americans.

The principal occupation of a cavalryman in Cologne was exercising racehorses. During the war, whenever the regiment was out of the line, they had spent their time collecting racehorses. Every officer's charger was in fact a racehorse, and we shared this school of horses with a certain gunner battery, who were friends of ours. Between the two of us, we had pretty nearly all the racehorses that were any good in the Rhine Army, and we certainly always knew which were likely to win, or (which was just as important) what was certainly going to lose in the Cologne races. It was the only time in my life that I ever made money on a racecourse.

Riding racehorses at exercise is a very different matter. For one thing, the more you pull at the racehorse's head, the faster the bloody thing goes. It is very hard to stop them. I became distinguished as the subaltern who was more often carted by his mount than any other. People, of course, were not very kind to you. One was most unmercifully ragged. I have never forgotten the time—in fact, the only time in my period with the Ninth Lancers—when I tried to sing at a concert. We shall cast a veil over that; it was awful. The reason was that two of us had decided to do a duet, and we did know the words, but the sergeant's mess got active before we came on and filled us up with a mixture; I think it was beer and whisky, but I am not quite sure, though I know it was the most god-awful mixture. We managed to get on the stage somehow, but we had no words left. My friend got off before I did, leaving me in the middle, speechless. It was not a very good beginning for a subaltern, but no one seemed to care very much.[3]

Ireland (1920–1)

Unfortunately, the next year, things were boiling up in Ireland, and we were suddenly sent over there. We were sent to a part of County Roscommon, where, in fact, very little trouble had been happening, I think very stupidly, as far as our lords and masters were concerned, because after our arrival, trouble started. It was not started by local Sinn Feiners, who were only boys anyway, and indeed played football against us, including one or two very dirty matches. Yet gunmen, a couple at least, were sent down from Dublin to stir things up. Shooting the occasional policeman from behind a hedge was about as much as anybody had done by way of Sinn Fein in recent times in that part of the world, and the chaps who got shot were usually those who were thoroughly disliked by local farmers. Farmers drove each other's cattle—that is, they would drive them off a farm and leave them widely distributed all over the county, but that was mostly personal spite rather than politics. The local Sinn Fein club was far more scared of the Dublin gunmen than they were of us.

However, the arrival of the regiment soon changed all that. An unfortunate factor was that our arrival was not so good for the few local gentry. My squadron's officers were billeted in a large country house, a very lovely house in a very beautiful estate with lovely gardens. It was owned by a war widow, a still young and very attractive lady.[1] On our first night there, we dined with our hostess. She produced a marvellous dinner, the cellar was opened, and pink champagne flowed. On the second night, it was the same, more pink champagne, and on the third, my squadron commander objected. 'If you go on being so hospitable, Madam, my boys will soon have drunk your cellar dry!' To this, her answer was, 'And why not? The sooner you get on with it the better. You won't be here for more than a few months, and as soon as you leave the "Shinners" will burn the house down. I know that will happen. I've been warned.' We were moved, and the house was burned, a beautiful house, with the most beautiful garden I have ever seen anywhere in this world. The lady had done nothing. She had to entertain us, *force majeure*. She had no option. We were billeted on her. That was Ireland in 1919–20.[2]

I did not care very much for my stay there. It was not much fun. The regiment was half recruits, so we really couldn't do anything, That half could not ride. They were in fact Welsh miners who had been sent to us, God knows, because somebody in the War Office had discovered that miners had pit ponies, therefore naturally they must be horsemen. Not one of these boys had ever seen a horse to ride it. They could sing, and that was all. Sing they did, beautifully. As a result of that, all we could do was take our horses out to exercise them, going out by one route and coming back by another, so as to avoid getting caught between hedges. It was not very funny. Several of us did get shot up. My best friend of that date was Tony Tennant, a member of a large country family and very knowledgeable on some quite esoteric country matters, such as hawking. He owned several hawks and had them with him. They were beautifully trained birds, and it was marvellous to go out with Tony. The birds were wonderful to watch. They came to hand so beautifully. They were quite tame with him, although not with anyone else. Tony got caught from behind a hedge and died. That upset me considerably.[3]

War is nasty, but civil war is even more so. For in a war, you at least know your enemy, but in a civil war, you do not. He can be anyone. Any corner boy leaning up against the local pub might have been out the night before on the game. We had spies, of course, but that reacted in a curious way. It was discovered that a local Anglican parson, who seemed a very nice chap indeed, had guns and ammunition concealed under the bedding in his house. He had to be arrested, and I fear his chances were not very good of escaping execution. It is worth noting it was not the Catholic priest, who might be expected to have some anti-British views, but the Anglican parson. Yet Ireland is a muddle. I had about a year of it, and then I sent my papers in.[4]

I had already come to the conclusion that the Ninth Lancers, the British Cavalry, was not for me. I did not have nearly enough money and no country estates in the background. We were not what you would call a rich regiment exactly, but a regiment of what were known in those days as country gentlemen, with pretty big backgrounds as far as estates were concerned, or younger sons of well-known county families, mostly from the West Country—a very nice crowd. Yet it was quite obvious that I could not remain. Rumour had it, and the rumour was correct, that the regiment would very shortly go to Egypt. I obviously could not afford it, and I could not ask my father for more cash. He gave me a small but reasonable allowance; I think it was about £10 a month. It was good enough for a subaltern in those days in an ordinary regiment, but nothing like good enough for what we were going to face when we went to Egypt.

I had to form up and tell my father that it did not seem likely that I could afford to stay in the regiment. He said 'Well, you had better go to a cheaper one, or go to the Indian Army.' I did not like the idea.[5] This was very stupid of me. I ought to have done so. Yet I thought, 'If I have to leave my friends, if I have to start again, and learn new ways and new tricks, well, I think I had rather get out altogether.' I am not very fond of peacetime soldiering anyway. There seemed to be very large gaps when nothing went on, and in an infantry regiment, these might be boring. Also, I was not of a warlike disposition at all. I got on well enough at Sandhurst, but that was principally because the Sandhurst discipline was very harsh and protected one from being bullied. At Harrow, I had been intensely bullied, so I was glad of the protection Sandhurst discipline afforded.

So I came to the conclusion that I must go elsewhere, and I had been reading at that time about orange-growing in South Africa. There were two very obvious advantages about this. One was that the fruit, Christmas being in midsummer, ripened at the opposite time of year to the European fruit and so would not be up against it in the market. The second point was that commercial growing of orange trees for export had not been done in any great way in South Africa before the war. So everybody would be starting more or less on an even footing. A third point was that my father had some very useful friends in the Genetical Society, and they, of course, would have their connections in South Africa.

Cavalry

Except for the Guards, whose *raison d'être* has little to do with war, there is no cavalry left; indeed, there has been none since some date between the wars of 1914–18 and 1939–45. Cavalry was really obsolete by 1914. The last cavalry charge, in the Western World at any rate, was in 1914.[6] Yet although the machine gun had already sounded its death knell, almost literally, cavalry persisted in use until well after the First World War, as in fact did mounted infantry. The armoured car was, more or less, bound to use roads, or at least tracks. The tank was still in its infancy and very slow-moving. So cavalry, between 1914 and 1918, was used as a mobile reserve. It was not in the line—in the trenches, all the time, as was the less mobile infantry in that war. Yet it was used in particular to plug gaps in the line, its speed of movement enabling it to be held back until there was an approaching crisis, and then moved quickly in to reinforce that part of the line. So cavalry had its casualty lists, as long as anyone else's, because it was used when and where the battle was hottest.

Since it has gone, forever, it may be worthwhile to give some idea of what a cavalry subaltern's life was like in peacetime.

Early mornings were usually spent in exercising the carefully collected string of racehorses, or, if you were a troop-leader, your troop. After breakfast, there might be lance, sword, or rifle drill, for newly arrived officers and other recruits. These would not, normally, be carried out on horseback. Otherwise, there might be tent pegging, which consisted in riding, with a lance, at a wooden peg in the ground. If you were clever, and if your horse ran straight for the peg, you could hook it up on the point of the lance. Alternatively, there could be sword drill, exercise with the sword, aimed at strengthening the sword arm. If you add to all these a bit of cross-country riding, rifle shooting, and pistol practice, it is seen that the subaltern's day was full and active. Then, of course, there were 'stables'. You must know the art of grooming a horse, and it is an art, for the horse must like the process.

South Africa (1922–25)

I do not altogether class Natal in my day as quite the same thing as the Union of South Africa became later. Natal, in fact, was being rather difficult very shortly after I went out there. In 1925, there was a thing called a flag bill. This was really centred on what flag the South African nation would fly. They were still a colony at that time, and so that flag was the British ensign, but the question was how much Union Jack should be on the flag and what else, if anything else. The Dutch (and one cannot blame them; they had been there for several centuries) did not want any Union Jack on their flag. When I went out there at the beginning of 1922, memories of the South African War were still quite good. Memories in a country like South Africa are very long, and in the case of the Dutch backvelder very long indeed. The backvelder was a farmer, who was usually more or less without any education. He had simply taken what land he could ride round on a fast horse in a day.

There came a time when the more sophisticated people of the Cape threw out the less educated farmers. They in their turn founded the Orange Free State, and, for a while, everyone was happy. Yet there came a time when there were more educated people in the Orange Free State and also less educated; again, the same thing happened. The more sophisticated people threw out the others, so they crossed the Vaal and founded the Transvaal. This fortunately, or unfortunately as you like to look at it, contained gold mines. These, of course, caused mad rushes, mad attempts by all sorts of people to grab what they could. People came from far and near to take part in the gold rushes. A gold rush consisted of lining up those who wanted ground and letting them race each other and peg out their ground. In the latter end, the Transvaal became extremely rich with the gold. The diamonds were mostly a little bit further west, at Kimberley.[1]

Yet, of course, there were many uneducated farmers, Dutch mostly, still left, and these people had failed to take advantage of what was there. They were the poor Dutch, and once more they got out of it. Probably there were a certain number of criminal types among them, but on the whole, they were just unlucky because they were uneducated. They in turn had again to trek, and the last trek was over the mountains to Natal, and in Natal, the Dutch farmer was always what was called a back-veld farmer. He was usually a very uneducated man, a very stiff and hard man, and very hard to deal with. If you visited a back-veld farm, it was very difficult to say who was what because there were so many multi-coloured people. The back-veld farmer took the local women and used them. So quite a bit of the population would be half-black. That might have worked in other parts of South Africa, but it did not work at all in Natal because Natal was originally Zululand, and the Zulus are a very proud nation indeed. The one thing a Zulu did not like was having his women tampered with. A Zulu woman in my day cost fifteen head of cattle, if she was a virgin intact. If she was not, she had more or less no value at all. The great idea among the Zulus was first of all to marry, but you were not allowed to marry until you had killed a man in battle. This was a little bit before my time, of course. Then you were allowed to marry, having shown your prowess. Having married, you bred girls. When my first child was born—a boy, Michael—the local natives came around, not to congratulate but to commiserate because I had produced a boy, not a girl. A girl was saleable. Several girls would set you up as a cattleman. You need no longer work, and gradually, as you increased your family, you sold the girls. The boys looked after the cattle, and, in due course, they became young spearsmen in the old days of the Masai and the Zulu. They became fighting men, and in due course, having killed a lion or a man, they were allowed to marry, put a ring in their heads, and become in their turn *indunas*. An *induna* was a fellow who did no work anymore. He just sat back and collected—a very pleasant, reasonable system, really. It worked awfully well until the white man came. The Zulus had conquered practically every race they came up against, except perhaps the Matabele, but there was very little difference between a Zulu and a Matabele.

When I went out there, Natal was still very largely inhabited by a pure Zulu population. Zululand, the northern part of Natal, spreading inland for several hundred miles, was separate. White men were not encouraged. A few storekeepers were allowed to be there, but you could not own land there. The Murray River, which ran into the Tugela, was the boundary. On the other side, it was purely and absolutely native Zulu. On our side, the south side, white men were allowed.

I was in South Africa from early 1922 to Christmas 1929. One reason for going there was because I imagined that one rode everywhere on a horse. In fact, in that part of Natal, where we finally settled, it was very hard to keep a horse alive at all. Unless it was immunised against horse sickness, it would die of that. Immunisation worked in only about 50 per cent of cases, and it was expensive. I did manage to keep a pony for about half my stay, but the sickness got her in the end.

After looking around for about six months, we settled on the border of Zululand, on the south side of the Murray River. We did so because we thought, and rightly as it turned out, that the settlers, mostly ex-Indian Army, took their farming more seriously than some of the other orange-growing schemes. The place was in the Low Veld, a country of deep valleys lying at about 2,000 feet. It is covered thickly with low scrub and thorn bush. These valleys, cut out by the rivers, are carved into the general plateau, at about 400 feet, which lies between the sea coast and the high mountains some 60–100 miles inland.

It is very pretty down in the 'Thorns'. At the back of my fence, there was a water furrow, and beyond this, there was a native location; no white man was allowed there. This had a most beneficial effect on my property because I realised very quickly that the local native was an extremely easy fellow to get on with. I was only twenty-two when I went out there. I found no difficulty in getting on with him, although I could not even speak his language at first. Yet as long as you paid him his standard wage of ten shillings per month, he was quite happy. If you gave him a little extra occasionally, if you managed to rig a feast—that would be meat, which was a rare luxury to him; there

Jack in Natal.

must always be a good reason for it, of course—he was your blood brother, or pretty nearly. The Zulu is a strong, brave, and by nature happy creature, and he had not, as yet, been poisoned by communist ideas. In 1922, the Zulu had respect for the white man.

I only ever during my stay had to sack one man, and that was at the request of his fellows. Only a few months after our arrival in the valley, when I had begun to clear ground for a house, employing some twenty or more Zulus, we lived in a building next door to the store. This let a room or two and was known as the pub. It was owned by the storekeeper, a Jewish Dutchman, who disliked the British. The shadow of the South African War of some twenty years earlier still hung very heavy over South Africa, albeit less so in Natal than elsewhere, since the majority of the whites in Natal were British. In parts of the Transvaal, they would spit and leave if you went into a bar.

I had to get over to my plot of land by sunrise. My workers came at that time and I had to set the tasks for the day. I had about twenty working for me, all round where the house was going to be built, at that time taking stones out of the ground, digging around generally. It was on a hillside, so there was quite a lot of levelling to do. One day, I was delayed at the building site and so got back late for breakfast, which was from 8–9 a.m., when I had already probably been up for an hour or two, because my boys arrived at sun-up. It was necessary to be there to set them to their daily tasks. I had a head-boy who spoke some English, but I could not rely on him. I had to be there myself every morning at daybreak. It was rather nice going to the site at that time because I had to cross the *sproot*, which was the tributary to the river, just below where I was living. This was almost in a cavern, because the walls of the stream were all over 20 feet, and some of them 30 feet high. The *sproot* itself had so little water that you could get across dry-shod with a few stepping stones. Yet it could rise 20 feet in twenty minutes, given a bad storm somewhere, not necessarily where we were, but further up in the mountains. So, one learnt to be careful of it.

The Zulu houseboy refused to bring me any breakfast, so I told him to 'go see his *baas*' and tell him that I had been delayed and wanted my breakfast please. He returned waving a knobbed stick, saying '*Baas* say get out, no breakfast'. The knobkerrie is a weapon, and a well-known rule was that weapons of any sort must not be brought into a white house by a native. So I told him to put it down, but he would not do so. So, I took it away from him but got a goodish crack on my forehead in the process of doing so. Fortunately, the stick was old and broke. I still have the scar. That was just as well for me because otherwise, I would not have been here now. I hit the boy in the stomach, which was the weak spot in a native, and he doubled up and ran off into the bush. Rather groggy and madly angry, I was pretty well berserk and bleeding profusely, so I went across to the store, probably with the idea that I would kill the storekeeper. It transpired he had given the kind of instruction to his boy that no white man gives about another white man; at least, you did not then. He had told his boy to 'take a stick to him'. However, fortunately, there were other whites in the store, and so I was prevented from carrying out my idea.

Of course, we had to leave. I removed myself and my family, and we went up to the local town, but that was 40 miles away. However, an acquaintance suggested a solution and I found a small cottage. It was just two round huts (*rondals*) stuck together under one roof, which was about halfway between Greytown and the Golden Valley where our property was, about 15 miles from there. The owner was quite agreeable to our moving in. He said it was a labour camp; that was a house built by a white man but entirely occupied by blacks as a source of labour, not used by the white man at all. It had been abandoned some years before. There were no ceilings. We had to put up ceiling cloth, which is rather an interesting thing because you can see what goes on above it, rats, mice, snakes. The snake is quite clearly differentiated from the rat or the mouse. There is a sort of wriggliness in his movement across a ceiling cloth. Everything, of course, peed through the ceiling cloth, but that was not very important. Africa is not a very clean country, unfortunately. We lived in that for about six months while my house was being built. In the meantime, neighbours got rid of the storekeeper by refusing to buy from his store. That was kind on their part. I think, in a way, my wife and I were pets of the community because we were considerably the youngest. After my affair with the store, the storekeeper, much to my surprise, felt boycotted.

But there was an even stranger result, and that was immediate. When I came down the following day to start my boys off at daybreak, I was astonished to find that all my boys had arrived there wearing only their thin skin *moochies* between their legs (loincloths), instead of the usual pair of dirty pants.[2] They were oiled all over and painted with streaks of white paint. They all had their large Zulu war shields and assegais, a forbidden weapon, but winked at for hunts by common consent. They were very noisy, making speeches, and they greeted me with a great shout. I asked the headman, who spoke a very little English, what was up. Was it a hunt? He said 'no, they come to burn down the store'. It took me a lot of time to persuade them not to do this. In the end I gave them a feast, to celebrate something or other, but first I declared a holiday and we had a hunt, to excuse the spears. I think we caught something, which no doubt provided the feast.

However, I was amazed since these boys had only been working for me for a very few months. What loyalty! It was some weeks before I was told that they were all in debt to that Dutch storekeeper. I learned later that it was an old trick, practised mostly by the Indians—we had one up the road and one down the road—and also by Jews in the back-veld country, to let the native run up a debt, usually for his wife, or his girl, for their clothing. The girl would want this or that, and the boy did not have to pay, so that was fine. Later on, he would have to work it off at a much-reduced wage. The storekeepers did extremely well.

Our arrival at our new and temporary abode was rather spectacular. We drove down, from the local *dorp*, Greytown, a small *dorp* with one 'hotel', which had yards of hitching posts outside. Cars were few there then, and horses were the normal. Our open Ford was loaded with everything one could need, pots, pans, a wood stove, etc. The road was only so-called for the sake of politeness. Rounding a bend in this track and nearly at our destination, we were halted by an alarming sight. Lining the road, on either side, were Zulus in full war paint, shields, spears, and all. They were oiled and painted and wearing huge, feather headdresses. There were some forty or so of them—an awe-inspiring sight. When we came in sight, they let out a shout, a roaring sound like the 'Banzai' (acclamation) used to greet chiefs, but we did not know about that, and it sounded more like the sort of noise one might have before a massacre. I halted the car. Then, up the middle of the 'road' came a strange creature. In a way, it looked more like an insect than a man, and I do not know to this day what sex it was. I think it was probably female, but it was impossible to tell. Smallish, dressed, if one could call it that, in shreds and tatters of dark nature, all bits and pieces that shook, menacingly, and most nastily. Little bags of skin hung from its waist and rattled drily. It carried a jumble of favours, trophies, and things to keep out the devil. It was the local witch doctor. It was sexless, and it was most horrible. It carried some sort of a wand, which it waved in menacing fashion. It seemed to mutter, but one could not be sure of that. Arrived in front of the car, it performed some curious antics, part of which was the strewing of something very disagreeable on the ground. It shook its stick or wand at us, cried some kind of greeting, slipped aside and almost vanished into the thick bush. The men then let out a great roaring shout. I concluded that the party was friendly, and we passed slowly between the two rows of menacing spears and to our new home. I still sometimes have nightmares about that.

The news of the arrival of a new white owner had penetrated the community. News travels very fast in the back-veld in Africa. It is conveyed by shouting from one valley to another. All that part of the world is very mountainous, and when you are down in the low veld at 2,000 feet, the high veld at 5,000 feet appears to be mountain peaks. It is only when you get up there that you find that they are really only cliffs, and behind is the more or less level back-veld. That runs back to mountains, which go up to another 5,000 feet, the Drachensberg being about 10,000 feet altogether. The welcome was to show respect, and was also an excuse for the new *baas* to give a feast, which we got organised with all speed. It proved quite expensive, for Africa in that day, but there was much hilarity, and it was well worthwhile.

Our experience of the Zulu proved very happy, and so long as his, or her, tummy was full there was very little grief among us. When it came to the girls—we had two for the house, when it became habitable, and a nanny for Michael, who was born in December 1922 in Durban, but almost on the road thither—none of these had been in a house, white or not, before. They were like children and needed watching, like children, but they were very good girls.

Our house faced the river, and the 30-acre orchard was below, between us and the moor. On the far side was a cliff, surrounding a large *koppie* (head or hill), which was very steep-sided and rocky, where a tribe of baboons lived: one could see them with field glasses. There was a leopard or so over there. It could probably catch the odd baby baboon. Yet we never saw it. The rocks also held pythons, quite a few of these. Collectors for such places as the snake park at Port Elizabeth would come and catch them. Their method was simple; you tethered a young goat on a wire. The snake would come and swallow the goat whole; a snake's upper and lower jaws are not joined except by elastic muscle, so they can swallow quite incredibly large things whole. They then go home, or just stay put, for a week or two, digesting the meal. So all the collector had to do was to gather up the torpid python and stuff it into a sack, not giving it time to vomit. Once inside a sack, the python gave it up and went to sleep.

Michael Richardson in uniform.

There was wildlife enough around our house, but one saw very little. There were *leguaan*, big aquatic lizards 4 or 5 feet long, living in the rushes by the river. These sometimes came up and stole our hens, as did the wild cats. A wild cat will, out of bloodlust, kill every hen in a hen pen. So we kept Runner ducks, which object and make much noise when being attacked, and lay good eggs, while hens get too frightened even to cackle. There were a lot of snakes, two species of cobra, one, the more common, being far less dangerous than the other. There were puff adders, very nasty, because they will not move and are very well camouflaged. We experimented with keeping a mongoose, African variety, but then found that cats—yes, female cats—are just as good at killing snakes, so we ended up with some fifteen cats. No snake came into the house, as there was always at least one cat with kittens to protect. A cat's method for fighting, say, a cobra is to crouch just out of its striking range. They tease the snake until it strikes; all it gets is a mouthful of fur—cats can puff out their coats to twice their normal thickness—but the cat is on to the snake's back and bites through its neck. I often saw this done, and never did the snake win.

If the Zulus were easy to get on with, the people of the South African Company, which sold our land to us, were less so. Yet the fault did not lie with them, as servants of a company whose shareholders were mostly shopkeepers in Maritzburg or Durban, who knew little of farming. The land, a lot of it, lying below an artificial water furrow something like 8–10 miles long, had once been an ostrich farm. The feathers had gone out of fashion long before 1914, the furrow had been made, and the land it served had been sown with lucerne. Yet that had not paid well, as we were some 30 miles from the railway. In 1918, some orange orchards were planted. The company had then been formed as the 'Golden Valley Citrus Estates', and shareholders were told that more land would be planted, the best of course, for the company every year. To finance this, land would be sold to settlers from the armed forces. These orchards would be managed by the settlers, but the fruit would be picked, packed, and sold by the company for a high percentage.

The first settlers were an engineer colonel and a gunner, who were very prudent men. They dug holes and found there was very little soil, so they bought land nearer the river, which had good alluvial soil. An orange tree likes a considerable depth of soil because it has a very long taproot. These two very early settlers were kind-hearted people, who warned anyone who came along and was introduced to them to take the precaution of digging holes and finding out what depth of soil there was. I did that. I hired two boys and dug holes in the ground I was first offered. Of course, that ground was useless, and finally, I found a plot near the river and its confluence with the *sproot* from the mountains, where there was a good 40 or 50 feet of alluvial soil. When I got there, the oldest orchards were about four or five years old and bearing fruit. So, one could get an idea of what was possible.

I bought about 30 acres of good land, and 10 acres of poorer land. Yet the poorer land was on a hillside. It had beautiful views, and that was where I put my house, about halfway up the hill, and in due course laid out orchards and gardens round it. The house was unusual for that part of Natal because it was not a collection of *rondals*, or a square house with a tin roof. You had one or the other, according to what you were going to use for the roof. The idea was that the natives could only thatch a round house, or at best two joined together. My design was in the shape of a 'Y', and I was solemnly warned by many of my neighbours that that was impossible to thatch. I had however observed that the local native thatchers were extremely clever, and I did not see any reason why they should not thatch a Y-shaped roof. In fact, they did. I had three thatchers on the three arms of the 'Y'. They all met in the middle. I offered a prize for the best thatcher. There was no best thatcher, so they had a feast. That thatch lasted for the next twenty years. For all I know, some of it may still be there. No one has ever complained of that roof.

My Y-shaped design produced a very unusual-looking house, the main *stoep* or verandah being between the arms of the 'Y', looking out over the valley. It was really very charming. On one arm was a dining room and a large sitting room, on the other was a double bedroom and a nursery. Michael, my oldest son, was born after we had been out about a year in Natal. He grew up in the arms of Zulu nannies. The Zulu nanny is very good with children. She is trustworthy and, on the whole, very careful. No snakes or spiders get near, and that is the main thing.

The incoming settlers, well advised by those already there, would only buy good land. So they got it, but the poor quality or shallow land was planted up for the company. The shareholders did not know. The promoters of this adventure were two Jewish gentlemen from Johannesburg, called Mr Rosenbaum and Mr Lax.[3] Mr Lax was the one with whom one dealt. Mr Rosenbaum was merely in the background. They held a large stake in the company but sold out quietly two or three years before the true nature of the business was discovered. This was not too soon because the first lands planted for the company had been no good. Yet they had left, pockets filled, before the facts were known. The company discovered that a lot of its land was worthless. It would never bear any marketable fruit. The company could not afford to meet its obligations and went broke. So we, the settlers, got together—there were about ten or a dozen of us, living on the spot, and some twenty or thirty still in the Army, whose properties were managed by those who were there—and we formed our own company.

We built a packing shed, bought the latest sorting machinery from America, and were the leaders in the formation of the South African Citrus Exchange, an organisation which made shipping rules, to prevent bad fruit going into the ships, and organised the marketing of the fruit in Europe. We purchased lorries. By that time, we had a motor road from Greytown down to the valley, and things had become very much more civilised. Our packing shed was quite successful.

It all worked well, but it did mean hard work. I looked after my own thirty-acre orchard, of some 2,000 trees, plus that of an absent neighbour, still with the Army—one had to prune every tree every year—and I also became the head sorter, which was a very responsible job in our packing organisation. I had three white assistants and two white women overseers of the packers, who were all women. It was entirely up to me and my sorters as to what went out for export by ship, and what was to be sold in South Africa or used for making commercial orange juice. By several years, I was the youngest of all the settlers, but we were all friends, and it worked.

Our household staff were all raw Zulus, meaning they had never been in a white man's house before, with the exception of the cook, who had worked as cook's boy in a home near Durban. There he had learned to make good bread, and what he called fairy cakes, which were fairly edible.

There was a reason for this. When I was building the house, the local missionary, a German of some sixty or more years who ran the German Lutheran Mission in the valley, came to have a look at what we were doing. Curiously enough, he was almost the only white man who thought that my design of a Y-shaped house, enclosing a big *stoep* in the arms of the 'Y', would work. The missionary strongly advised me not to get any of my workers, especially not any women, to work in the house from his mission. This advice shook me somewhat. He explained that the Zulu, in his or her habitat, lives by strict rules. The girls are valuable, their price, as wives, being then about fifteen head of cattle. Yet, he said, the boys and girls who became baptised as Christians left all that behind them. They put on European clothes and aped the whites, but without understanding. God must never see a naked body in church or out, but that did not prevent you stealing out to meet a boy. They were children, who learnt the new religion very, very slowly, but they had discarded the old rules, so they had no rules. 'The raw people from beyond your water furrow will be far less difficult to keep in order. They will obey your rules, when they know and understand them.' That was how it turned out. The fathers of our girls would come at least once a month to chew a little bit of tobacco or smoke a pipe, to talk with the *baas*. Very polite, their visit always included a quiet session with the daughter, to make sure that she was still at least technically a virgin and had not deteriorated in value. The girls themselves were bawdy enough in their speech, especially with any of the boys, but they took a great pride in their own value.

South Africa (1925–9)

In 1925, my parents, who had been out in South Africa for a year or so, agreed to come and keep our house warm, while Delia and I went home for a month or so.

As things worked out, my mother soon went back to a civilised hotel, but my father liked having the garden to play in, and so he had started a series of plant experiments. I had arranged with another settler to run the orchard. Some of these were seedlings in boxes, which he had told the garden boy to water morning and evening. One evening, there was a thunderstorm and my father was horrified to find the boy watering the boxes in the pouring deluge. Result: no seedlings and a sacked garden boy. The cook also got the sack for coming into the house drunk. He was not, in fact, drunk but high on *dagga*, which is hemp and smoked by Cape Coloured boys. They came to the Cape originally to work in the fishing and canning industry or became journeyman carpenters, bricklayers, and similar semi-skilled workers. Cook boys, who were often trained in some household near a town, would acquire the habit from the Coloureds. So, on our return from Europe, we found our cook, who could make good bread and some sorts of cakes, had gone to the police camp nearby, where he was allowed to smoke as much hemp as he liked, provided he did so in his own hut, which was outside the police camp fence.

Incidentally, to give you some idea of the cost of living in Europe in 1925, Delia and I spent a month in France on £100—we had not a penny more— going to Paris, Avignon, Arles, over the Italian frontier to some small place just to say we had been to Italy, Carcassonne, and Lourdes, where we joined a group of pilgrims from Belgium, then went, in procession, to see the famous Virgin in her miraculous grotto. We had arrived at Lourdes rather late at night and were horrified to find in the morning that the hotel was named the Hotel of the Immaculate Conception.

We ended our trip by staying at my uncle David's new house in St Jean de Luz, and then, of course, at my uncle Selby's in neighbouring Ciboure, to tell them about our stay at David's. We travelled by train, by day, on the hard seats of the third or even fourth class. We ate very well but did not wash overmuch.

After some years, our orchard came into bearing and, because the house was better than most and in a nice garden, we got a good offer for the farm, which we accepted, and returned to London.

My farm in Africa was a success, and God knows why. I think probably because the original choice of what to do was worked out reasonably well. When I was wondering what I should do if I left the Army, I came upon some pamphlets about the future of orange-growing in South Africa. They were, of course, fairly commercial, merely selling land or property, but there seemed to be a line of truth within them. I felt that this had something reasonably good. I looked into it and found that the orange-growing community of South Africa quite clearly did not know a damn thing about growing oranges commercially. Oranges had been grown commercially in Palestine and Spain for centuries. They were grown now in America, particularly in California. My father knew about plants, fruit, etc., because that was his fun and games. So, we collected information about orange-growing, particularly in California. It seemed to me that if I went to South Africa with knowledge collected from California and other places, I would be in a position at least equal to anyone else since no one prior to the war had done anything about exportation of fruit from South Africa. Yet exportation from South Africa, or any place of that distance, was now perfectly feasible and reasonably economical. You could strike the market in Covent Garden, say, or Berlin, and the prices you would get, minus the cost of your shipping, would be equal to that of oranges coming from Spain or Palestine. So it seemed to be a reasonable proposition, and so it turned out.

My orange farm was a success. When the trees had come into full bearing, I was able to sell it at a good profit on what I had paid for the original land, and what was more, my house. My house really sold the property because it was quite unique in that particular part of Natal. I had taken a great deal of trouble building it. It was a very nice, pretty, and comfortable house, and it had a most magnificent view. I do not think the people who bought it ever regretted it. Well, I was lucky to get away with it. I was going out to South Africa with no knowledge of the country at all, except that you could ride a horse anywhere, which was complete nonsense.

England:
How I Got Involved with Cierva
(1929–34)

We intended to go back to Africa, perhaps up to Rhodesia, and buy a larger area of orchard land—we could not expand where we had been living—but the gods decreed otherwise. Our marriage did not stand the test of living under civilised conditions, perhaps because we had been starved of them in South Africa, and so now over-ate, as it were. Perhaps, too, we did not really both want to return to Africa. We were no longer the same two inexperienced kids who had gone out seven years before. So, we split up; I then lived mostly in France, because it was cheap there, and I had to give most of my small private income to pay for Michael, who had schools to face.

I had now to find myself a job, a very hard thing to do at that time, even if one had any qualifications, since there was at that time what was known as 'the Great Slump'. Firms, large and small, had gone into liquidation everywhere; it was worldwide. There was nothing to be found. After some two years, during which I would earn nothing, things began to look rather grim. I was eating into my small capital. Then I found an old friend of my father, one of his close skiing and sailing companions. Toby Wroughton ran what was called the London News Agency.[1] This dealt in press photographs. They lent me a camera, an enormous Reflex affair. When I asked if I could not have something smaller, they said: 'No. Your job will be to go to such places as Hurlingham or Ranelagh to take photos of the young lovelies whose boyfriends are playing polo. If they see that camera they will know that you are Press. Knowing that, they will form up, with boyfriend, so that you can take a picture of them!' So it was.

Yet, at such places as Hurlingham, I would run into chaps who had known me in my cavalry days, who sometimes ragged me about my new profession. So, one day in 1931, I decided to try aviation and went down to an airfield outside London (at Heston), where the Guards Flying Club was located. No one was likely to know me there, but there might be lovelies there too, and there were a few. Yet, also, there was a thing called an Autogiro.[2] This was a peculiar kind of flying machine, having a large windmill-like rotor above it and small stub wings at each side. I examined this creature and talked with its pilot. The machine was having some difficulty in getting off the ground— there was no wind—because, the pilot explained, you had first to get the rotor spinning above a certain speed. This rotor was not driven by anything, but once the necessary number of revolutions per minute (about 250) had been attained and you were in the air, the rotor would continue to turn at around that speed of rotation, owing to the flow of air over its blades. The aircraft was either being dragged along by its propeller, or gliding and losing height. The machine could not stop still, so there was always a flow of air to keep the blades rotating. On this machine, the rotor was started by pulling on a cord wrapped around its hub. If there were any wind to help it to do so, the rotor would be blown round at an increasing speed, until enough revolutions had been attained. Then the machine, which had been held fast by brakes, was allowed to move forward and would take off. I later saw this done, and was very impressed by the way the machine could be handled once in the air, even at very low forward speeds. With power off, it would glide, losing height quite slowly, and the final touchdown was almost vertical, with no run after landing. This landing impressed me very much, for this aircraft was obviously much safer than the ordinary aeroplane, which had to land with considerable forward speed in the event of engine failure (common enough in 1931), or running out of fuel. I had a talk with the pilot, who was getting rather tired of showing the Autogiro and decided he was going to grow pigs instead, which I believe he did, with great success.

It would be just the thing in Africa, where the bush was often too thick for a safe landing. Many farmers, especially those in wool or sugar, were quite well enough off to own an aeroplane, but few would take the risks entailed by the impossible country over which they would have to fly. There was nowhere you could force-land an aircraft anywhere in the neighbourhood of Durban, or within about 100 miles of the coastline. They had absolutely nothing to spend their money on. They bought a new car every year and would take it along to Durban, and that was that.

Juan de la Cierva was born in 1895 in Murcia. He became Spain's first and leading aircraft designer at a very early age, and, by 1919, he had built several aircraft, including the first three-engined machine in Europe. This unfortunately crashed on its first trials, killing the crew. The crash occurred at or just after take-off, one of the most frequent forms of accident in those days. Cierva immediately gave up designing fixed-wing aircraft, and turned his attention to rotary-wing, at that time represented only by helicopters, which rarely succeeded in leaving the ground, and were completely unsafe if they did so.

The cover of Jack's scrapbook:
30 Years (or so) of this!
1932–1962.

Señor Juan de la Cierva.
Photograph in Brie, *The
Autogiro and how to Fly it*
(1935).

By 1922, he had succeeded in flying his first Autogiro. Unfortunately, early Autogiros had no means for starting the rotor, other than such primitive methods as a cord wound round the fan mechanism. The reason was quite simply that no one could build a clutch sufficiently strong to take the strain of starting the rotor continuously, and at the same time light enough to be capable of being used in a light aircraft.

By 1922, however, the principle of auto-rotation had become quite firmly established in everybody's mind. A number of people started playing with the idea, several others in Europe and America. Cierva's first successful machine was shown in Spain around 1922–3, and he got a great deal of praise for it but no financial support. That was forthcoming later, when Air Commodore James Weir brought him to England and obtained the backing of the Kindersley family and Lazards. That financed a small company, the Cierva Autogiro Company, which was patent-owning, and the first British-built Autogiro was built by Avro under licence from them. This still had no means of connecting the engine to the rotor, and therefore still had great difficulty in starting, especially under no-wind conditions.

At the underground station, I bought an aeronautical weekly, *The Aeroplane*. In it, there was a leading article by the editor, C. G. Grey, on the subject of the Autogiro, which slated it as being an aircraft that would never get anywhere, because no one would want to bother to learn to fly it. It was a fair enough article, designed, of course, to promote discussion and printable comment. One of the points made against the Autogiro was that although such machines had been flying for several years, the ordinary potential customer, if such in fact existed, could not learn to fly one *ab initio* (from scratch). He would have to learn to fly on an ordinary aircraft, e. g. a Moth, and having been to that amount of trouble, he would not then wish to relearn the Autogiro technique. Not only would it cost him much more, but by that time he would have, in most cases, learnt to enjoy the more versatile capabilities of the ordinary fixed-wing aircraft. This criticism, emanating from such a source, set me wondering, for what I had seen had impressed me.

The next day, I visited the office in Bush House, Aldwych, of the Cierva Company, using my press card as an introduction. I asked the company secretary if he had any comments to make on the *Aeroplane* leader. He said that indeed he had. They expected to start training *ab initio* pupils within the next eighteen months. By that time, they would have perfected a sufficiently light but strong clutch, which would enable the rotor to be driven up to beyond its required flying speed, while the aircraft was held stationary by its brakes. A combined release mechanism would then enable the pilot to release both clutch and brakes simultaneously. Since the rotor would have attained its auto-rotational speed, the forward movement of the aircraft would maintain that, and take-off would be possible with only a very short run, even when there was no wind to assist it. They would then start a school to train pilots *ab initio* on their own machines. So I said to him, 'Right, you have your first pupil. Please take my name and inform me when you are ready to start.'

I then went home to my lodgings and thought. The private pilot's licence could be granted by any properly qualified instructor. Cierva's had such a person. Based on experience of instruction on a Moth or similar light aircraft, the number of hours flying would be somewhere between fifteen and twenty-five. The price of flying in a gyroplane had been quoted as seven pounds per hour.[3] So a private pilot's licence could cost £100, more or less, but of what use would that be to me? If I wanted to sell Autogiros in South Africa, which was then my idea, I would need far more experience than twenty-five hours, as who would teach the potential purchasers?

To do anything worthwhile, one obviously needed to become a professional and instructor. To do that would require a minimum of 100 hours of solo flying. With one thing and another, it could hardly be done at less than 150 hours total from the start—a lot of money to me at that time. Yet if and when I was ready to take the commercial pilot exam, who would examine me? There was, as yet, no officially qualified pilot at Farnborough, nor had they any Autogiro on which to examine me. Also, they could not use an ordinary aeroplane. Then, the idea came; they must be able to examine me. The rules did not allow for such a situation because it had never occurred. It would be a farcical situation and they, the powers that were, would have to alter the rules. It would be excellent publicity for Cierva's.

The leading light of the Cierva Company seemed to be Jimmy Weir. Since he lived at or near Glasgow, my uncle Bob Mackenzie (Sir Robert Mackenzie of Edinbarnet House, near Glasgow) would know him. Uncle Bob was the colonel of the Highland Light Infantry and a chartered accountant very well known in Glasgow. So I wrote to my uncle Bob and he contacted Weir, who liked the idea very much. It was agreed that I should go ahead as a first pupil and get my 'A' licence, paying the score for that. Then I would continue to be instructed and would do the necessary 100 hours solo, payment to be delayed to later. After gaining my 'B' licence (the commercial one), I would be taken on by the firm as an assistant pilot and could pay off the cost of my training out of my salary. There were three of us on the first course on the Autogiro. We started on 5 August 1932. Tests were taken on 12 September, and I was granted my 'A' on 13 September.

At that time, Cierva's had two professional pilots, both of course very experienced on ordinary aircraft, both ex-RAF—Reggie Brie, who did most of the demonstration work and was also flight manager, and Alan Marsh, who had taught Cierva to fly an ordinary aeroplane (Moth) a year or two earlier and who was the test pilot and chief instructor.[4] Any licensed pilot would have to pass instruction by Marsh in order to get the Autogiro included on his licence. Cierva insisted upon doing a first-ever flight on any new and un-flown type of his design, but after that he would hand it over to Marsh. He and Cierva got on very well. When Marsh had tested out the machine, he would then hand it over to Reggie and brief him as to methods of flying it. Reggie would then get to work and perfect his technique, until he could literally make the machine sit up and beg. He was a very fine demonstrator. Marsh was a very nice chap indeed, with the faculty of inspiring utter and complete confidence.

On my arrival at the Cierva hangar, at the Hanworth Club outside West London, I saw a rather alarming sight. It was an Autogiro fuselage minus the rotor, seemingly wrapped around by an electric cable. I was told that Reggie Brie had been practising take-offs in the White City Exhibition Arena on the previous day and had got his tail-fin hooked into a lighting cable. The machine had come to a dead stop in the air and had then slowly subsided on to the side of the stadium below it. The rotor had been broken up, but otherwise, there had been no very crucial damage, and Brie was quite unharmed. The story was substantiated a few minutes later when I was introduced to Reggie Brie. Fate, it seems, was determined to convince me of the safety of the gyroplane. It gave me enormous confidence. If a thing like that could happen to a gyroplane, and the pilot could just walk out as Reggie had done, there seemed to be a future in this toy.

'Alan Marsh and Reginald Brie in front of an Autogiro school C.19 Mk. IV at Hanworth', from Brooks, *Cierva Autogiros* (1988), p. 113 (with kind permission from Miss E. A. Brie).

Less than a month after I started my course of instruction, I was taken by Marsh to assist at a demonstration he was giving at some air show in the Midlands.[5] Alan was to demonstrate the aircraft and put it through its paces, and then we would stand by for anybody who wanted to fly in it at five bob a time. I should see they were properly seated in the aircraft, help them in and so on, wipe up the sick if any were sick, and receive any half-crowns which they happened to give me, which, he explained, the flight staff could use for beer later. This was thought to be good experience for me. Our return to Hanworth was to be on the following day.

After the usual, satisfactory, engine test we took off, but as we approached the high hedge at the edge of the field, the engine died. The hedge was a thick one of trees some 20 feet high. Marsh pulled the nose of the aircraft up hard so we lost all forward speed as we hit it. We fell, slowly, down into the hedge as the rotor blades chewed their way through the branches, until there were no blades left. We were both quite unharmed, if a trifle shaken, and managed to climb out of the aircraft and down to the ground. In no other aircraft would we have survived that accident; so much for the safety of the Autogiro. It seemed to me just about the safest thing you could get into the air at that date, and from then on, I had reason to be wildly enthusiastic about it.

The three of us on that first gyroplane flying course were the first *ab initio* pupils on gyroplanes, I believe, in the world. One was 'Jeep' Cable, who had been in the London Messenger Service.[6] His place on the course was thanks to an arrangement with the Commercial Cable Company. He later joined Cierva's and became a professional pilot. He was a very good pilot indeed, and went to the United States during the war. He became one of the first and best helicopter pilots in the USA, later the leading RAF helicopter test pilot. He was killed in the Air Horse accident in 1950.

The other candidate for a private pilot's licence on that first course was an elderly gentleman (McMullen, aged about sixty-eight), who told us that he had a nephew to whom he had taught the arts of fishing and shooting, and much more by way of sport. That nephew had recently got his wings in the RAF and was boasting that, at last, he had done something Uncle could not do. McMullen had a very strong Irish sense of humour. So he had tried to learn to fly a Moth, but the course had not been a success. He had agreed with Cierva's that he would buy an Autogiro, provided that they would enable him first to obtain a private pilot's licence. He said nothing to his nephew about what he was doing. He got his licence in due course and the Autogiro was delivered to him, and he flew it to his nephew's airfield, 'just to show him that I am not on the shelf quite yet'. Arriving, he said: 'Here is something which you can't do.'[7]

The Cierva Company at Hanworth consisted of two small hangars, located at the side of the island, which was the centre of the airfield. The airfield was

The Author and his Auto-giro.

J. A. McMullen and his Autogiro, the frontispiece to his book *Simplified Aerial Navigation by Dead Reckoning* (London, 1933).

Aviator's certificate for John William Richardson, 13 September 1932.

a large, round open area, with a small copse, a garden, and a clubhouse in the middle. The atmosphere was extremely friendly and rather amateurish. Cierva himself was an extremely pleasant, fattish man of around thirty-seven at that date. He was usually laughing, and he was very much liked by the staff, particularly by the mechanics with whom he worked. The production aircraft were being built by Avro, but a certain amount of work was always on hand at Hanworth itself. This small concern was almost like being a member of a family.[8]

I was a slow pupil. This was partly due to my eyesight, which (although I did not know it) was lacking in binocular vision to some extent. This made landing rather trickier than it would normally be. In 1933, I finished my necessary 100 hours of solo flying. One could act as an assistant instructor or safety pilot without having obtained a commercial pilot's licence. Provided that the chief instructor was present, he did not have to be in the aircraft. An assistant instructor was not allowed to teach or interfere with the pupil. He was there to take over if the pupil got into a mess. Farnborough, having no pilot trained in Autogiros, sent one of their examiners to us. After some dual flying with Marsh, he was sent up with me, as safety pilot. When I reported that he seemed to be fine, we changed seats, and he examined me. I am afraid that none of us took matters seriously.

To obtain a 'B' licence, one had to do a night-flight between two specific places. The Autogiro had never been flown at night (at least in Europe; I do not know about America), so Marsh and I did a couple of flights after dark to see if there was any problem, but there was none. We then notified Croydon Airport that I, a candidate for a 'B', would be carrying out a night flight that evening, giving the registration of the aircraft, but we did not say that it was an Autogiro. Marsh came to Croydon with me after dark, to satisfy himself that it would be possible. At Croydon, we made the usual Autogiro approach. The Control Tower officer saw our lights coming in and then starting to sink almost vertically. This so alarmed him that he ordered out the fire engine. This cost Marsh a few drinks at the bar, after I had gone on my way to Lympne on the coast.

The actual examination flight, by night, was without any incident. It was a fine night. One could see quite a long way. There were the lights of London and the lights of railway lines, railway stations, and so on, and finding my way down to Lympne was completely without incident. There was no difficulty whatsoever. The flight took three quarters of an hour. It was, I think, the first official examination flight by night conducted on a gyroplane or any other aircraft of that type.[9]

Another first was a blind flying one. That came a year or so later, when the requirement came in that all commercial aircraft should be capable of being flown blind, and all commercial pilots should have complied with a blind flying examination. We never in fact flew the early gyroplanes blind for any other reason, but the front seat of one of them was duly fitted up with a hood, and with Alan in the back seat, I was instructed as to how to navigate the aircraft. Later, I made the first official test, which consisted in flying the aircraft blind under a hood, with a safety pilot behind to take over in case anything went wrong. Nothing did go wrong, and I was able to find my way quite easily. Yet it was an interesting experience because when you fly blind for the first time, you realise that there is a fallacy in the old idea that your bottom is the thing that tells you which way up you are. That is complete nonsense. It does nothing of the kind. Only your instruments can do that, and if you rely on any other notions you will very soon be what used to be called 'arse upwards'.

We managed to keep the press in ignorance of the B licence lark, so as not to embarrass the authorities, but the story got around and caused a good deal of amusement. Also, it was good publicity. So, I was granted my 'B' on 4 September 1933, the first to be issued for a gyroplane.

Around about this time, Reggie Brie went to Italy and gave a demonstration before the Italian Navy authorities of landing on the afterdeck of a cruiser. He actually demonstrated landing and taking off from this, both of which worked perfectly well. It was a little dicier than it sounds because there is quite a lot of gear around the afterdeck of a cruiser, which could not easily be removed. A platform was built and space made for the aircraft to get in, but it was a tricky procedure. Reggie carried it out perfectly. He was at his best always when giving this kind of demonstration, but curiously, he was not of the kind that makes a good test pilot.[10]

My position had now become a sort of assistant to both Reggie and Alan. So far, all my flying had been on the C.19, MK IV, which had stub (i.e. short) wings carrying ailerons (for lateral balance) and a tailplane with a rudder and elevator for steering and fore and aft control, all operating as in any ordinary aeroplane. These controls were fine at ordinary flying speeds, but of course, the Autogiro did not depend upon forward speed, since the rotor could not stall, as a wing would do at speeds below the critical. Yet an Autogiro could be pulled up to a complete stop in the air in perfect safety. All it did was to sink vertically at a speed too high for a safe landing, but completely in control. It was only necessary to put the nose down, to turn this vertical sink into a glide. If there was a wind of over about fifteen knots the final touchdown could be made to a dead stop; if less, there would be some very short run. However, at these very low forward speeds, control became sluggish, owing to lack of airflow over the control surfaces. Very slow landings were increasingly tricky if there was little or no wind.

There was also a C.24, of which only one was built. That was a cabin machine built by de Havilland. It was faster than a C.19, had a larger range, and was in general a cleaned-up improvement. The only trouble was that it was extremely noisy in the cabin. This was Cierva's special proud possession, and no one else apart from Marsh and Brie was allowed to handle it. However, towards the end of my training, I was allowed that honour too and flew it quite a bit. It was a remarkably easy machine to fly.[11]

Cierva C.24 Autogiro G-ABLM. It appears to be warming up before a flight, with the propeller turning, but not the rotor (from scrapbook).

Flying for Cierva (1934–6)

Meanwhile, Cierva was perfecting the next improvement to provide full control, even at nil forward speed. This was to remove the stub wings and the tail elevator and rudder, and to control all movement fore and aft or lateral, simply by tilting the rotor. He had been playing with a C.19 fuselage from which all ordinary control surfaces had been removed, but the rotor head (i.e. central hub) could be tilted in any direction. The revolving rotor would follow the tilting of its central hub. This provided complete control, fore and aft, and lateral, absolutely regardless of the speed of the aircraft. With this control, forward speed was unnecessary, and the aircraft could be dumped vertically, even with no wind at all. If you were not sure of the type of ground, you could let it down gently the last foot or so, as I once had to do later in Spain, when landing in a bog. This development resulted in the C.30 Autogiro, known by us as the Wingless Wonder.

I had my first flight in the C.30 on 3 May 1934, with Cierva himself at the controls, followed by some dual flying with the French test pilot Lepreaux and Marsh, and meanwhile gave joy rides to visitors to our hangar. On 13 July, I did my first solo on the Wingless Wonder; after that, I flew that aircraft (the C.30) until the war, and later, in 1943, in its service version. It was a quite remarkable aircraft. It did, however, still require some forward run on the ground, before take-off in conditions of little or no wind. Cierva was still perfecting the next step (the 'jumping giro') when he was killed. The C.40 came into service in 1938 and became a practical part of Flight 1448 at Duxford in 1940.

When I joined the firm, there was no one else on the flying side, but after I had qualified, they took on another chap as assistant to Marsh, who had done a great deal of flying on ordinary aeroplanes, and of course had to do a conversion on to the gyroplane. His name was Yates, and we did a number of flying jobs together. He was a Lancashire lad, who had never been out of England, and had flown during the first world war. Dr James Bennett was Cierva's assistant and worked most of the time up in Glasgow, where there was a small secondary firm, which was busily working on plans for a complete helicopter.

I was now a full member of the Cierva team, but by this time, I had developed my skiing technique to the point where I could be certain of getting a job either as a representative of the Ski Club of Great Britain—I was a judge for first-class tests—or running a racing club, or both, and so get free railway passes and free board and lodging at a first class Swiss hotel for several months. This was too good to miss since I loved the mountains and skiing. The British climate reduced the amount of flying we could do in winter, and an assistant was not required at Cierva's. So I came to an arrangement with them that I could take three or so months off in winter, unpaid, on the condition that I be contactable by telephone and available to return, if required, at short notice. This made life perfect, and I went off to Switzerland for three months. The arrangement worked very well. In 1934–5, I did several jobs for Cierva's over Christmas and New Year, including one to Switzerland, but got away from February until May 1935.

I had also found the antidote to life on an airfield. My job, as assistant pilot, was mostly demonstration (I was learning to be a fully qualified instructor but did not qualify until mid-1935), some foreign deliveries, and a lot of joy-riding for visitors to Hanworth. This, of course, packed up in bad weather, when we often shut up the shop. Unfortunately, bad flying weather, rain and poor visibility are common in England even in high summer. However, I had friends who were working artists. They shared a studio in the building in Pimlico where a very fine painter, McNab, ran a very good art school.[1] I had done a little work in the Heatherley School, in London, before I started flying. Yet the Heatherley was commercial and full of very young students. I learned very little there, except that a career as a commercial artist was very uncertain, and that it was not what I wanted. But I had learnt some of the basic rules of art. At McNab's, I was allowed to use a corner of my friends' studio whenever I wished and also to use the facilities of the school for a small fee. These consisted in a life class in the mornings or all day, and a composition class on certain afternoons. There were, too, afternoons when students would be given a subject, usually some sort of event, and thirty minutes in which to illustrate it. A visiting artist, often well-known, would be invited to criticise the results. I was rather good at the latter, and often got praise for my sketches. My main trouble was that my drawing was poor, although my ideas were often good. It was, however, all good fun and better than mooning about at Hanworth in the rain.

Most of my time at Cierva's after I had qualified was spent instructing. That is rather a dull business on the whole, but it has its interesting spots.

Spivs, a caricature by Jack.

For example, I had two Indian gentlemen to teach for a time. They had come over with a Maharajah who played cricket. He was a very considerable cricketer apparently, and his object in interesting himself in Autogiros was that he was going to buy one in order to be able to fly from one cricket ground to another in India. His father, he told me, was middle-aged, old for an Indian, and would not last very much longer. The trouble with them is they die off young. I don't know whether it's diet or what, the way they live.

Two of his chaps also were taught, so that there would be two available pilots to fly the gyroplane from cricket ground to cricket ground, when he himself was going by other means. These two fellows, nice though they were, proved extremely difficult pupils, I think probably because they were terrified. They had a habit of freezing at the controls when anything unusual happened. I asked Alan Marsh what I ought to do under these circumstances, and he said, 'Take a long needle and stick it into his bottom when he freezes.' The chap would be in the front seat of course. One hardly liked to do this to a pupil, but it was very difficult and one spent a good deal of one's time creating situations in order to promote the freezing and get past it. These situations could sometimes be rather dangerous, if freezing continued too long and one did not take over.[2]

Of course, the foreign deliveries were the real plums of the game, the reason being very largely that, wherever one went, the Autogiro had never been seen. It was an unknown creature in Europe. No one else was building them there, excepting one or two experimentally perhaps in France and Germany.

In America, Pitcairn and Kellett were both using Cierva patents, and Cierva very often went over there. Whenever there was a new model coming out, he always insisted on going over and making the first flight in it. That was one of the endearing things about the man.

The newness of the gyroplane, particularly in Europe, also meant that wherever you went, you were treated almost as a VIP, certainly as a most privileged visitor. You met people whom otherwise you would never have met at all, and one was entertained considerably. You had of course to repay this by giving the odd demonstration, but that naturally was not frowned on by the firm; in fact, it was very much a part of your job. One had a few tricks to show off the aircraft, which perhaps the ordinary pilot would not have used. One was a special landing when you turned the aircraft downwind, crossed the airfield low down, helped by as much wind as there happened to be, at an apparently very high speed, which was probably not much over 100 knots, but because of the lowness of the aircraft seemed much more. Then you cut the engine. You were downwind, in an impossible position to land in an ordinary aeroplane. One did what was described as an 'Immelmann turn'; you turned practically on to your back and at the same time slewed the aircraft around so that its nose came into the wind, it lost all speed, and you dropped vertically on to the ground. It was quite an easy trick—simply fly past, gather all possible speed, cut engine, do Immelmann turn, and land. You could not miss, but it did look quite good, and it always caused the spectators to stop breathing for a moment or two.

My first foreign job (between 30 August and 5 September 1934) was to deliver one of our C.30s to Bata, the international cheap shoemaker in Prague, Czechoslovakia, and to put it through whatever tests the authorities there might require. Bata had sent over one of his own pilots—he had a small fleet of aircraft—to learn the tricks of flying our aircraft, but he was not allowed to touch the controls until the aircraft had been accepted by the Czechs. He flew entirely as my passenger. I think he wanted to get somebody in his organisation used to the idea of rotary wing, so that when the helicopter came along, as no doubt it would, they would be ready for it. Obviously, that was going to be extremely useful to a chap who sold boots all over Europe.

Our flight was uneventful until we reached Frankfurt. Then we sprung a leak in the petrol tank and had to return there. We felt pretty glum, since to repair a petrol tank could take some time, and it was already after 2 p.m. In England, no one would be allowed to put a flame on to it (probably essential) for forty-eight hours. A young Brownshirt (Nazi) was sitting at the airport café near to us. He came over and introduced himself, saying that he had seen our Autogiro go out and then immediately return. Was there anything wrong? He spoke in excellent English. I told him our trouble, and he said: 'Would you leave the matter to me to see what can be done?' I agreed and went with him to the hangar with a mechanic. The tank was taken out in a matter of minutes, and then a long black open Mercedes (beloved by the young Nazis) arrived, and we were driven into the outskirts of Frankfurt, to a factory building.

There a worried-looking official was waiting on the steps. My young companion said something short and sharp in German and ended with a '*Heil* Hitler'. The other '*Heil* Hitlered', the tank was removed, and we left. It was now about 4 p.m. Our conductor then took us to a hotel, where, after a drink, he left us, saying he would let us know later what was happening. He rang up a little later and informed me that my tank would be back in the aircraft before morning. There would be no charge, as we were regarded as guests at the airport. '*Heil* Hitler'.

So, we were in the air by 6.40 a.m. the next morning, headed for Nuremburg, Karlsbad, and Prague. I have to admit that this little piece of 'show off' was impressive. It would have been quite impossible anywhere else. It demonstrated the complete and ruthless power of the Nazis, but we were most grateful to our host.

My business in Prague was simple enough and took little time. The sale had been made by an agent, one Dick Malone, who flew out in his firm's Gypsy Moth. Dick was a very good pilot, who worked as aircraft salesman for Henly's of Piccadilly. Henly's dealt in cars but also in aeroplanes. Dick came out to deal with the business side of the sale, to get the cash. He had too some other interest with the firm of Junkers at Dessau in Northern Germany, so we flew there from Prague. At Dessau, I was left alone to my own devices for several hours, during which I wandered about the factory, which was fairly full of Brownshirts, but no one bothered about me, so I even went into some of the hangars. There was a large aircraft on the tarmac outside one of these. It carried obvious bomb racks. It was probably a Ju 52, the type used six years later for bombing London. Junkers built civil aircraft, of course, but I did not think they were allowed to build bombers, as yet. So when I got back to England, I talked to an acquaintance at the Air Ministry, who said 'Oh yes, we know all about it, but no one nowadays seems to care.'[3]

From Dessau, we went to Leipzig for the night, and the next day, we set our course for Cologne, but we ran into very nasty weather over low mountain and forest after about an hour's flying. The cloud was right down on the hills ahead of us, and as we had no radio, we could not know what conditions were at Cologne so dared not go up above the cloud. Dick decided to get out of the hilly country by going north, and I gave him a course for Kassel. Arrived there we found great activity both in the air and on the ground, with light aircraft, and squads of Brownshirts. We were told it was the Sporting Flying Club having a Gala, but it looked far more like a military exercise. We enquired about the weather towards Cologne and were told that it was good, which we knew to be untrue. We assumed that we were rather unpopular.

We had arranged to pick up a friend of Dick's at Cologne, so Dick did some telephoning, and then told me that instead, we were to go to Hanover and spend the night at a friend's home, which was in that neighbourhood. We had no trouble between Kassel and Hanover, where we were met by a very ancient limousine, driven by a very severe-looking uniformed chauffeur.

Now, I have to recount a most strange story, and, in a way, horrible, being set in the scene of Nazi Germany in 1934. It was not very long after Hitler had come into power in 1933 and 'the Night of the Long Knives', which took place in summer 1934.[4] A few days before we flew to Prague, Dick Malone went to a party in London. At that party, he met a young German, Hans von Herwarth,

From Jack's logbook (record of flights), recording his flight to Prag via Germany (30 August–1 September 1934).

From the logbook, recording the return journey from Prag via Germany (3–5 September 1934).

who was more or less weeping into his cocktail glass. He told Dick that he had just left his ancestral home in Germany, to return to New York, where he had a job selling pictures and *objets d'art*. He was now waiting for the ship, which would carry him across the Atlantic. His people, he said, were far from being Nazis. His mother was the ex-wife of a Prussian general.[5] His stepfather was also a general and hated the Nazis, but he thought he could make use of them. His sister, who was very beautiful, and of whom he was very fond, was being pursued by young Nazis, most of whom believed that women were for their particular pleasure. So she was pestered to sleep with them, and how could she hold out for ever? 'We are too old-fashioned, and can't, and won't, kow-tow.' He feared for them, that he might never see them again.

To this, Dick said that he was going to Prague, via Germany, in two days' time and would not be away for more than four or five days. When would the ship leave and where was his home? The ship would not leave for ten days, and his home was an old castle near Hanover. Must he stay in London? No, he had finished his business there. So Dick arranged to take him in his aircraft, drop him off at Cologne, and pick him up there on his way home from Prague. Dick had, in any case, some business to do at the Junkers factory at Dessau in Germany. It was done, but Hans omitted to warn his family. So, when he walked into the hall at Schloss Seerhausen, his sister, who was coming downstairs to see who had come in, saw him and fainted.[6]

Schloss Seerhausen, the castle near Leipzig where Jack stayed on the return flight from Prag, 3–4 September 1934. This postcard with the carnation was sent to Jack after his visit by Renata Herwarth von Bittenfeld, the stepdaughter of the owner (from scrapbook).

The *Schloss* was magnificent, the dinner was delicious—partridges from the estate washed down by a very good pink champagne—and the sister was quite one of the most beautiful things I have ever seen. The general, who was retired, was an excellent host, and the party was a cheerful one.

At the end of the meal, our host insisted on our drinking large balloons of some special brandy. Nerved by this, I asked him what he and his kind thought of the political situation. He said: 'We don't particularly like it, but anything is better than the Weimar Republic, which couldn't govern at all. The Nazis are being very brutal, but they have got the young men on their side. Youth is being bribed to be tough, selfish, and brutal, and to have all the girls it wants, with no holds barred. If you are good at any sport you will be encouraged and helped. It is giving the young men back something they had lost since our defeat. But we in the Army will watch it and prevent it getting out of hand. Hitler is a bounced-up little man, but he can talk. We won't allow him to get out of hand.' I think he nearly believed this.

Hans explained matters rather more clearly the next day, when we were on our way. He said that his stepfather, and his own family, had owned some excellent shooting in Bohemia before the last war, which of course they had lost. 'We think it just possible that the Nazis might get this back for us.' Hans' stepfather was a proud old Prussian. When, after the 1918 defeat, he married Hans' mother, their best friends besought them not to make a show of it, for fear of public reaction. Yet neither he nor she paid any attention. The general wore full uniform with decorations, she dressed to kill, and they were driven from the church in an open carriage, and the people cheered them.

I was given the haunted room to sleep in. The ghost was a lady who walked about 2 feet above the floor. The room had once formed part of a larger ballroom. However, I was too tired to wait up for the lady. The next morning, Hans came to wake us early and took us to see a very special sight. In the high wall, which surrounded the garden, there was a breast-high opening, with a shelf, which extended outside and could be closed by a shutter. There was a bench outside, and several poorly clad people were sitting on it. This, Hans said, had once been the place where lepers (common enough in the old days) were fed. There were no longer any lepers, but the custom of feeding the very poor had been kept up, this despite the fact that the *Schloss* was nowadays only kept alive by selling flowers, carnations in particular, at the Berlin market.

It really was a most beautiful place, in a state of charming dilapidation, which rather enhanced its charm. I could well understand why Hans felt so unhappy. Later, I received a card from his mother, with a warm invitation for a further visit, and another with a dried carnation stuck into it, from the sister, to say that 'Mother always means what she says'. However, I never went back. That might have had its dangers, and not from the Brownshirts. I never heard what happened to them.[7]

So we said goodbye to the ladies, but the general insisted on coming to the airport, very erectly seated, and looking dead ahead when we were stopped by Brownshirt police at the airport entrance. There was considerable delay in getting the aircraft out of its hangar, which was not explained at the time.

We had an uneventful flight home via Antwerp. Both Dick and Hans seemed very thoughtful until we were over the Channel. Then they cheered up, and Dick explained that the wings, which could be folded back, had hollow spaces at their roots, which were filled with papers, which it might not be wise to keep at the *Schloss*. When we reached home, some of these were actually shown to me. Hence the delay at Hanover, as there had been someone in the hangar. I tremble to think what would have happened to us if they had been discovered. Well, that was Nazi Germany from all angles in 1934. Comment is hardly required.

My next foreign job proved how uncertain was flying in small aircraft at that time. There were two of us (the other was Yates) to deliver two C.30s to the Spanish Air Force in Madrid. It was impressed on us before we left that the essential thing was to get both aircraft to where we were heading, not only in one piece, but completely unscratched. The paintwork must be in perfect condition on arrival. We could only carry enough fuel for about 250 miles, so, for safety, had to plan our flight in steps of not over 200 miles. Yet in December, weather could often be quite impossible for small aircraft, especially if not carrying a wireless.

We left on 7 December in the afternoon. We left so late because of very bad weather reports on the coast. We had to spend the first night at Berck. Our route was via Le Bourget, Orleans, Tours, Poitiers, and Bordeaux. In France, we met with every kind of bad weather, bad visibility, rain, and, towards the coast of the Bay of Biscay, very high winds. It took us three nights to reach Bordeaux. We found that Yates' aircraft had some engine trouble at Bordeaux, so he had to return to Bordeaux and spend two nights there. At Biarritz on 12 December, we found no information at all, except that three French Air Force-type planes were expected, daily, from Burgos. We were stuck in Biarritz from 12 to 23 December.

During that period, we made four attempts at crossing the Pyrenees. These mountains are not so high at their western end, but they are steep and rocky, and wild enough, with deep valleys. We met winds of 100 knots on some of their ridges, and our own maximum speed was only 95 knots. At one ridge, I saw an eagle; it was hovering in the up-wash at the windward side of the ridge. My clock showed 95 knots and I was standing still. I swear that bird looked up at me and winked. It put its head down and disappeared into the valley ahead. I could not follow it.

On that, or some other occasion, I was unable to cross a ridge and got too low and into the down-current on its leeward side; it was a head-wind. It was as if I was in a waterfall; I had no control, was more or less upside down, and almost on the rocks. I do not know how or why I got out of that, washed out by the down-wash of that great wave of air. I had just got clear of those awful and far too close rocks when I saw Yates. The same thing was happening to him, and his aircraft was nearly upside down. This rather pleased me because I knew that he was an experienced and very competent pilot, so it was not, after all, just Jacky's fault. However, we were both very lucky.

On 23 December, we crossed the mountains and landed in Vittoria, to find the French service pilots at lunch, on their way back to France. They had much more powerful machines and carried radios, but they had been stuck in Burgos for a fortnight. They had tried flying above the clouds but had been unable to get down safely to land, so had had to go back to Burgos. We were invited to the local barracks for lunch and afterwards, I was shown around it by one of the officers. The rooms in which the men slept were indescribably filthy. When we went down to the stables below, there were mules and reasonably clean straw. There seemed to be a lot of muleteers about. My showman said, 'These chaps come down from the mountains, and they prefer to bed down in the stables, rather than going up to the sleeping rooms above.' I could hardly blame them.

That evening, we made it to Burgos, to be stuck there too, for another five days. We were warned, in Burgos, that the weather over the Sierra de Guadarrama, north-east of Madrid, was quite impassable for us. So we attended the Christmas Midnight Mass in the Cathedral and commended ourselves to God. I dragged Yates to see it. This very much alarmed him. All those people in cowls, I must admit, did look a little bit fierce.

On 28 December, we set out for Madrid in very poor conditions. Yet the Sierra de Guadarrama proved quite impassable, with the passes all in thick cloud, and probably also at Madrid. About half an hour before Madrid, I was running out of petrol and could not return. We lost one another, due to cloud, but both of us found the same large patch of green in an otherwise brown hillside. We both decided that the green was too green, so perhaps boggy ground. We both made vertical, no roll landings, which are tricky in a C.30 except in a high wind. There was in fact none, and it was raining heavily. We were right about the ground; it was boggy, and our wheels went well down into it.

We were wondering what to do next when some *Guardia Civil* appeared, well protected in mackintoshes. With them was a peasant. He bade us, by signs, as neither of us spoke any Spanish, to follow him and took us to a small village quite close by. We had not seen it in the heavy rain, as it was exactly the same colour as the countryside around it. Here we were greeted by the village priest, who was perfectly charming, and taken to his house. We were then given a meal and a bed. The priest spoke no French, so we were reduced to signs, until I remembered some dog Latin from my school days. This, rusty as it was, did help with the priest. Supper was rather like being animals at the zoo; we were seated in the middle of the room, at a round table with a hole in the middle and a charcoal stove underneath, which provided a very welcome heat. Elders of the village sat around us and commented, no doubt politely enough, but it was rather embarrassing, like being inhabitants of the ape house.

The next morning, we had a difficulty; we needed a loo but could find none. So, my Latin being inadequate, I was reduced to making a drawing of our requirement. This proved immensely popular. It was completed with much detail and presented to the village. We were then conducted by village elders to the bottom of the garden, where all was well.

We found our aircraft quite unharmed. We had covered them with some groundsheets we carried for that purpose. Two *Guardia Civil* were watching over them. They seemed to have been there all night, but would take no monetary reward, only cigarettes. We did not know, but found out later, that the village was on land owned by the Cierva family, and the priest had been in contact with Madrid by telephone. It was a nasty morning with a lot of low cloud, but our short flight to Madrid was uneventful. It had taken three weeks to get there, but the paint on the aircraft was unscratched.[8]

On return to London, which was immediate—we were requested to return, and caught a late train, on the evening express—and allowed me no time to see anything in Madrid, I had two trips to Paris for the French government, the first in a formation of four Autogiros, piloted by Brie, Marsh, Yates, and myself.[9] There was nothing eventful about that trip, but that night, I had an experience that shocked me. We were taken to a series of night joints, some smart, some sleazy, and one shocking. This was no news to me as I had lived in Paris for long periods, usually in Montparnasse because it was cheap there. However, it did manage to astonish one or two of us, being quite as naughty as they hoped. One such, an expensive and very well-known spot, where you could take your broad-minded wife, but which also provided for those in need of much lighter company, was known as 'the Sphinx'. It was about 3 a.m., but that did not matter to us, since we would not be flying next day but going by train. We ran into a couple of young men, known to us as recently joined pilots on a lesser airline (not British Airways), which ran a Paris–London–Manchester service. They were reaching a very obviously advanced stage of acquaintance with two very naked ladies of the house. We, of course, had no reason to concern ourselves about their pleasures, until one of them reminded the other that they must organise an early call, and then explained that they were due to take off for England at 8.45 a.m. 'The boss [this referred to a well-known and very tough character] expects us to fly in any weather. We have had a fog warning, but will almost certainly have to go, so to hell with it!' The passengers would not know, and after all, you can fly up out of the fog, but even so, it rather shook us.

Since BA or other respectable airlines would not accept inexperienced pilots, these had to get what they needed from the mushroom firms or charter people, who took them on at low pay rates. From some recent experience, I rather think that situation has not changed such a lot.

On the other trip I was alone and did not stop over in Paris.[10] For whom the aircraft were destined I have forgotten, but one was, I think, Bréguet, who had built a gyroplane of their own design. It would have had to use some of Cierva's patents. At that date, any country with any real interest in aviation was fielding its own version of the Autogiro. In America, there were two firms, Kellett and Pitcairn, both using Cierva's own designs, and he was often over there to confer with their designers. There were several firms interested in France, and two or three in Germany. As a result, our trips abroad could have very interesting sidelights. One was always welcome, and always helped in every possible way, and one met a lot of interesting people, whom one would not normally have met. Although one did not get so much pay, that was what made the job so very worthwhile.

That winter, they kept me busy up to the end of January. I was sent out to deliver a machine for the Swiss Government at Bern, and to give whatever training was required.[11] My route out took me to Strasbourg. I was refused hangar space in the government part of the airfield—the only occasion when I met with any difficulty from officials—but managed to get space in the local Aero Club hangar. There was a small crowd there when I landed, who had come to watch the French pilot Costes, who had recently flown the Atlantic, and who came from Strasbourg. My arrival caused some excitement, and I was invited to a party for Costes that evening; it was a very amusing and interesting party, with a certain amount of ragging and speech-making. So the next morning, I thanked my hosts by giving a demonstration before leaving. At Bern, there was a great deal of low cloud and some snow falling. I could not find the airfield at Bern Belpmoos and had to land in a park, which was a disused airfield. A policeman said that I had no business to land in a public park. I said that I was very sorry, but I could not stay in the air with no petrol, and I could not find the airfield. He was quite nice about it, directing me to Bern Belpmoos. Very much to his surprise, I turned the aircraft around and took off over his head.

I was there from 19 to 31 January. This was a very pleasant interlude. There were very thorough acceptance tests and much flying of officials, and I had to train the chief pilot of Alpar, the company receiving the Autogiro for the government. I had several others to train, all without difficulty except one, an official of the Air Office. Mr Gsell was determined to solo the machine, and I was warned that it was very desirable that he should do so, since he was probably the most powerful person in Swiss aviation at that time. Unfortunately, Gsell had only one eye, the other being glass. This meant that he had no binocular vision, which made it very hard for him to judge an approach to land at the very much steeper angle than that of a fixed-wing machine. Gsell told me that he had flown everything that had ever come to Switzerland, including a Zeppelin airship. He was certainly a very skilled pilot, but we had a lot of trouble, not assisted by some very rough weather. Both

Right: Schweizer Aero Revue Suisse (February 1935), reporting on the delivery of the first Autogiro to the Swiss air service (from scrapbook).

Below: Instructing at Bern (January 1935): Jack with Gsell (engineer), and Eberschweiler (chief test pilot for Alpar, the Swiss company who received the Autogiro for the Swiss government) (from scrapbook).

Gsell and Eberschweiler, the test pilot, took me on a demonstration of landing on glaciers in a Fiesler Storck (I think it was) anyway a quite remarkably versatile aircraft, with a very low landing speed and very short take-off run.

The Swiss press gave the Autogiro (the first in Switzerland) a very big coverage indeed. I finally managed to get Gsell off solo, which ended a very interesting and pleasant visit to a very charming and hospitable little city. Ah yes, and as they found out that I could ski, they took me out for a most enjoyable day in the high mountains. I went over from Bern to do my usual skiing job, at Wengen, for the next three months.

In 1935, a good deal of my flying time was devoted to doing the instructor's course. This was the ordinary course for a full instructor's ticket, adapted when necessary to the Autogiro. It was quite a long and quite a tricky course; one had to learn a patter—what to tell the pupil in various situations. I was in fact doing a lot of instruction already, but only as assistant under Marsh, whereas this ticket would enable me to teach *ab initio* pupils anywhere. Of course, I had been instructing pilots already, when delivering machines abroad, but that was allowable as conversion. One was largely acting as a safety pilot, to take over if the chap under instruction got into a mess. It was quite a different thing from teaching a man who had never flown anything before, and also a fully qualified instructor's signature on the pilot's log was accepted by the Air Ministry for the grant of a private pilot's licence, which was all that the average individual wanted.

Yet I had one job that summer that was interesting from several angles. It was to deliver a C.30 to the Italian Navy at La Spezia, then to remain there to train two naval pilots.[12] The flight down to La Spezia was interesting because wind conditions are often tricky for a small aircraft in the Rhône valley. That valley acts, at times, almost like a wind tunnel. It lived well up to its reputation, and my little Autogiro was rather like a leaf in all that wind. Arriving at Marseille I was rather tired and very nearly sat on top of an Air France liner, which was coming in to land. My descent had been far too vertical for the approach to a busy airport. Pilots did not expect to have to watch out for something coming almost vertically down from above them; their eyes, of course, were on the runway ahead. Fortunately, I saw him just in time. Yet I was very unpopular with the flying control and got out of Marseille Airport as fast as I could.

The only incident otherwise on the way down was my refuelling at the Italian frontier. The fuel is very suspect in such places, and I had a chamois leather with me and filtered all my petrol. It was just as well that I did because what was left on the chamois leather was no one's business. In such places, you find in the officers' mess rows of photographs, and when you enquire who they are, they are all people who have passed over; that is to say people who had fallen out of the air, and I suspect very largely because of the bad petrol used. Certainly, this was the case with the French Air Force in those days.

James Richardson by Sir Daniel MacNee. James, great-grandfather of Jack, founded the family sugar trading firm in Glasgow. Cf. Appendix I.

David Richardson of Hartfield, second son of James and grandfather of Jack.

Sarah Kimberley, the wife of Edgar Bishop.

Molly, an oil painting by Simon Elwes.

George Scott with portrait of his wife, a sketch by Molly.

Lord George Scott, an oil painting by Molly.

Jack as a baby, an oil painting by Henry Tonks.

Jack by Mabel Richardson, an oil painting (1929).

Guatemalan dancer in Paris, Señorita Graziella Andania. Crayon portrait by Mabel Richardson (1932).

Michael's mother, Delia Andrews, aged about twelve, a hand-tinted photograph.

Schloss Frens, near Cologne, where Jack was stationed in 1918–19.

Michael Richardson
(1922–2005), the son of
Jack and Delia, as a boy.

Cierva C.24 Autogiro G-ABLM in the de Havilland Aircraft Museum (London Colney, Herts). Photograph with thanks to de Havilland Museum/ Gary Lakin, and permission from the Science Museum (London), from which the C.24 is on permanent loan. This was the only example of this type that was made. It was flown by Jack between 28 April and 18 May 1933.

St Jean de Luz, an oil painting by Jack.

In Spain (Alicante?), an oil painting by Jack.

Cierva C.30 Autogiro AP 507 in the Science Museum, London. (*Science and Society Picture Library*)

Above: The Westland Heliport at Battersea, which was opened on 23 April 1959 (from scrapbook).

Below: Jack, in retirement.

La Spezia proved fascinating. It is a large naval base in a most beautiful bay, just north of the marble mountains of Carrara. There are several very charming little resorts scattered about the bay. Mussolini had recently declared war against Abyssinia and was about to launch an invasion of that country. La Spezia was the loading point for the troop transports. So, it was full of army wives, there to bid a tearful farewell to their husbands. Most of them were young and very attractive. This meant big business to all naval officers, for wives had to have support, wives must be comforted. Awful things were predicted for those unfortunate enough to fall into Abyssinian hands. They would be of little use to their ladies, should they ever return.

The Navy was too busy to bother, over much, with its new toy, and the weather was really very hot. So we only flew in the early mornings and had packed it up by 11 a.m. The drill, then, was to go to one or other of the reserved naval beaches. Lunch would occupy a considerable part of the afternoon. It was usually taken at a country pub, Italian version of course, and very different from an English inn, with more activity, more bustle, and with very good food. I have rarely eaten better, and never eaten more. After the pasta, the fish, a meaty main dish, a delicious ice cream and cheese, it was very naturally the hour for a siesta. The Italian Navy and local Air Force certainly did themselves extremely well. One might think about flying around 5 p.m., but that was also a good time for a cooling swim, and then there were ladies in need of support and comfort, and the Italian Navy must sacrifice its time and thought to this all-important matter. Very often, the evening would be spent at one of the outlying spots on the other

Jack (right) at Sarzana near La Spezia, in June 1935, where he gave instruction to pilots of the Italian Navy (from scrapbook).

side of the bay. There were many of them. An amusement then would be to sit in café chairs and watch the world go by, in twos and threes, girls together and chaps together usually. The girls were very lively. The great idea of our naval boys seemed to be to find out how many girls' bottoms they could pinch, keeping a regular score as it were. The girls did not seem to object very much. The bottoms waggled pleasantly past, and no one seemed to get very angry about it.

After ten days or so, we broke the aircraft, yet it was no one's fault; at any rate, no one at La Spezia was to blame as there was some small error when the aircraft was built, at Avro, outside Manchester. I was contemplating sending off my better pupil solo, but I decided, unfortunately, or perhaps fortunately, on just one more run with him. On a C.30 Autogiro, the wheel brakes held the aircraft stationary, while the engine was driving the rotor up to its correct speed for take-off. When this had been reached, the pilot pulled a small lever; this freed the clutch and, at the same time, the wheel brakes. This control was only at the rear seat and was not duplicated.

A pupil nearing his solo flight would be in the back seat, since this was the place from which the aircraft was normally flown. The pilot went through all the motions correctly, but when he threw out the lever, the clutch for some reason was not disengaged, but the brakes were. The aircraft began to move forward, and immediately started a violent and uncontrollable swing to the left. We took off in fact as if we were a helicopter, with a driven rotor, but no tail rotor to correct the violent torque. We landed, immediately, because I cut the engine to prevent our completely turning upside down, but we had gone over too far already, and so that was what happened. We hit the ground tilted at something around ninety degrees. The rotors broke up and we were on our back. I was hanging by my straps and could not get at their fastenings, and I had no knife. I could see a liquid, which could only be petrol, dripping past a hot exhaust pipe: fizz, fizz, fizz. Not a happy moment at all. It must have been several minutes before my pupil released me. I had to be cut out by him. Bar a bruise or two, we were both unhurt.

The aircraft was obviously a write-off. It could not be replaced because sanctions forbidding the supply of war material to Italy had just come into force. I could foresee a very unpleasant time ahead for me, probably in an Italian fortress. The airfield filled up very rapidly with a most extraordinary collection of top brass, but I managed to telephone our agent, explained the situation, and got back to my hotel on some excuse. I then packed my bags, went to the station, and caught the very first train to the frontier. I did not even wait to get my laundry. When we had passed the French frontier, my relief can be imagined. Mussolini's invasion of Abyssinia was extremely unpopular with most European countries, except Germany. The firm had been paid for the aircraft, and could not be allowed to supply another, so no one minded about this accident. I never heard any explanation of why that control stuck: why then and not before? The aircraft had done some thirty-five or more hours flying.

Cierva's Death and His Character

On 9 December 1936, Cierva was killed in what was accepted as an accident to a civil aircraft (flown by KLM), owing to engine failure on or just after take-off at Croydon.[1] I have never felt able to accept such a coincidence. Cierva left off designing ordinary fixed-wing aircraft because of precisely that accident, in 1919, which killed his test pilot and crew. It is so impossibly unlikely. However, Cierva was very heavily involved with the organisation of the military revolt against the Red Spanish government, which began the Civil War. Not only did he often disappear for long periods in 1935–6, when it was said by those who might know that he was in Germany, where he had some very good contacts with high officials in the Luftwaffe, but, in addition, he was one of the four people directly responsible for enabling General Franco to escape from Tenerife to North Africa. The account of this exploit is given in 'A Memoir of Hugh Pollard' published in *Blackwood's Magazine* (November 1973), pp. 459–61.[2]

This account states Cierva obtained the British Dragon Rapide employed to fly Franco from Tenerife and its pilot, so would it not seem that the crash was not due to accident but sabotage? Nowadays, this has, unfortunately, become almost commonplace, but that kind of terrorism had not begun in 1936, and baggage was not examined for explosives or weapons at a civil airport. The effect on the Cierva Company was disastrous, and it more or less closed down.

Cierva was of medium height, with a rather chubby face, dark, and good-looking in his way. He had a very pleasant smile and a very pleasant manner with all of us. On occasions when I was abroad, we might meet, and he would probably take me out to lunch. At these times, he was an extremely interesting companion, particularly on the subject of his own country. I got the impression that he was very royalist, but I did not realise anything like the extent of his royalism. He was in fact one of the leading lights in the preparation for the fascist rebellion. Of course, without Franco, there would have been no rebellion. He was by far the youngest general in Europe, and the only person who had the necessary enthusiasm and courage to carry out such an undertaking. Franco was also a highly intelligent man and thus able to avoid the pitfalls of fascism. I do not think Cierva would have backed anyone else because he was far too intelligent himself, but from what he told me, and from what I have myself gathered, through having relations who lived on the borders of Spain, the Spanish had had little alternative to getting rid of their royalty because their royalty did nothing for them. It had in fact become effete. Yet, on the other hand, no one excepting a royal person could really govern Spain. Historically speaking, Spain needs a hard-hearted dictator to govern it. It has to be kept in order. The Spanish *hidalgo* (gentleman) is for himself first and everybody else a long time afterwards; he himself and his family are what count and nothing else really does, his religion only perhaps to a small extent. Bull-fighting is something in which he is required to indulge as a boy. You will find in the south that most landowners have at some time been into a bullring, not necessarily public ones, but you have to display your courage. The southern Spaniard, the Andalusian, likes courage, physical courage, first and foremost. That physical courage can often be combined with cruelty is not a matter of any interest to him because to him, there is virtually no such thing as cruelty to animals. An animal has of course no soul in the Catholic religion, and so it does not matter.

Cierva did not quite have that point of view, but to some extent, he was a typical, very fine, and very intellectual Spanish gentleman of the first water. He was married into the champagne Codorniu family, and there was plenty of money on both sides. That was why he was able to give up ordinary aeroplanes and started what other people called messing about with strange ideas. His strange idea had been that there must be some way of keeping a rotor rotating, so that a rotary-wing aircraft could continue in safety when its engine cut. That was his discovery. Without it, there would not be a chopper flying now. That discovery was quickly taken up by others. There were several other gyroplanes, one or two quite satisfactory ones, flying in Europe and in England, and I believe more in America. At the time I joined the firm, there were two American companies: Pitcairn and Kellett. Kellett was in advance in my opinion with giros. When I went to America in 1944 to look at helicopters and report on their development, I went to Kellett's, where they showed me the gyroplane— 'which', to quote the test pilot, 'was streets in advance of anything we had produced in England at that time', the reason being that they had continued with that development for military purposes to a far greater length than we had. I expect the whole question really resolved itself into a cash problem. The Americans had much more money to burn on this sort of thing. The size of their experiment shocked me. There were at that time about six firms coming into production on various types of helicopter, and that was only in 1944.

Cierva's charm was very great, and he was sincerely respected by everyone working under him. I think that was because he always insisted on doing the first, most dangerous flight himself.

Flying in 1936–9

The next stage in the development of the Autogiro was the jump take-off. This had been done on an experimental aircraft, but it was very far from being perfect. The experimental aircraft was able, unaided by any wind, to make a vertical take-off or jump, but the height of the jump was very uncertain, and it was not certain that the aircraft would always climb away from the top of its jump. So it was unclear as to what height of obstacle it could clear. The experiment was continued, but not very fast or very wholeheartedly. This was possibly also due to the fact that the first successful flights by experimental helicopters took place at about this time. Focke-Wulf in Germany had designed and built a true helicopter, i.e. an aircraft obtaining all its vertical lift and forward speed from one or more driven rotors. This had two similar rotors placed side by side on lateral arms. It was given a public showing with much flourish of Nazi trumpets in front of Hitler, in the *Deutschland Halle*, Berlin, a very large covered stadium. It was flown by a woman, Hanna Reitsch. It was said by some critics that this venue for the public showing of this aircraft was chosen because it was sheltered from the wind, the degree of lateral stability of the machine being still, perhaps, a bit uncertain. It was also said that Hanna Reitsch had been chosen as pilot because she was the lightest available pilot.[1]

Be that as it may, the aircraft was developed into a larger and apparently efficient machine, which went into production during the coming war. Yet, as Focke himself said sadly, in a lecture to the British Helicopter Association shortly after the end of the war, we knew too much about that development and came over and bombed the factory, when the first batch of aircraft were waiting to be delivered.

We ourselves had an experimental helicopter flying at about the same time as Focke, but we said very little about it. It was built by a small team organised by Jimmy Weir, outside Glasgow, and Cierva had of course very much to do with its design. There were two versions, both with side-by-side rotors,

THE NEW AUTOGIROS

Advantages of the " Autodynamic" Rotor Head of New Weir Type : Jump-starts of More Than 20 ft. Altitude : Almost Any Field a " Girodrome "

It may quite safely be said that no single step in the evolution of the Autogiro has marked such great progress as the introduction of the direct-start, or " jump-start," principle. In Mr. de la Cierva's first British machine, it may be recollected, the rotor was started by hand, a cord being wound around a drum and a number of men running out " with the rope. The speed thus attained was not great, and it was necessary to taxi around the field for quite a time before the rotor speed was sufficient to take the machine into the air. The next step was the aeroplane tail, in which one of the surfaces could be tilted in such a way as to deflect the airscrew slipstream on to the rotor blades and start them moving. This was an improvement in that the pilot was able to start his rotor without outside help, but the rotor speed was still rather low. Then came the introduction of the engine-driven rotor head ; this enabled the rotor to be speeded up to the desired extent, and brought about the possibility of take-offs with short runs. At the same time, the suppression of fixed wings and the use

of direct control of the rotor head was a great improvement.

Last year Mr. de la Cierva announced that he had succeeded in making starts without any forward runs. In his lecture to the Royal Aeronautical Society he disclosed the fact that this was done very simply by merely sloping the hitherto vertical hinges in the blade roots. While the blades were being driven by the engine they lagged behind, and the sloping hinges had the effect of reducing the angle of incidence. so that the rotor could be speeded-up to almost any desired extent within reason. As soon as the drive was removed by declutching, the blades " caught up," and in so doing they increased their angle of incidence. The energy stored in the rotor was very considerable, and was sufficient to lift the whole machine several feet before the rotor had slowed to normal flying speed.

The new Autogiros, with those responsible for the Weir W3: 'from left to right, Mr. G. E. Walker, Mr. F. L. Hodgess, Air Commodore J. G. Weir, Mr. C. G. Pullin, Dr. J. A. J. Bennett ("mathematician"), and Mr. H. A. Marsh, who has carried out the test flights.' (*Flight*, 23 July 1936). The W3 was an earlier single-rotor type than the ones mentioned in the text (from scrapbook).

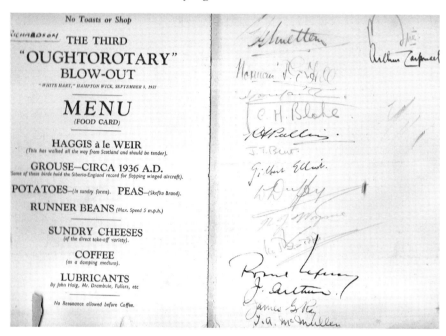

Menu of a dinner on 8 September 1937, with signatures (from scrapbook).

Charles William and Jack in 1937.

and very similar to the Focke-Wulf design. There was another helicopter development in France, by Bréguet. It was claimed in 1986 that this helicopter flew before the German one, but I am doubtful as to whether the Bréguet machine was a true helicopter. I know that they built a gyroplane and were experimenting with it.

After Cierva's death, I did only enough flying to keep my licences in order until the Second World War began. There were no more foreign deliveries of aircraft, and there was no work for me. Fortunately, I had recently got married to Eileen and had at the moment my hands fairly full with other matters. I did a little demonstration work over in Northern Ireland, at a large show that was organised by the then Director of Air, who lived in a large estate near Belfast. The estate was next door to Clandeboye, which was owned by Lord Dufferin, who had purchased one of our aircraft, but he was not a very good pilot. He did not want to demonstrate it himself, but he had promised that it would appear at this large garden party. So he got me to come over, stay a week, and do a demonstration. The result was so successful that I went back there again for another week later. Apart from that, there were no excitements at all.[2]

I tried to get taken on by the RAF, but I was coldly told that they did not contemplate using any Autogiros, and that I was too old to learn to fly ordinary aircraft. So I asked the War Office if they would put me back on the Army Reserve, which was done.

It is rather amusing to note that the RAF, a little after the war had started, got hold of every Autogiro in the country that could be made flyable, and would take on anyone with pilot experience of them. This was because these aircraft could do certain jobs better than a fixed wing. Their main job was rather a dull one, but very important, radar calibration—a very boring job![3] But there were chances of others of a more interesting nature. As it turned out, I probably had a more interesting and perhaps more useful war.

14

Skiing

I must put in a few words about skiing because it was through skiing that I met again my former close friend, Ronnie Macdonell, and was invited to return to my old regiment, should war break out. Without that meeting, I would have had no contact with that set of people and would probably have rejoined the Army, if they would have me, without making any attempt to return to my old regiment. I would have expected that it would take too long to learn to be any use in an armoured regiment. My invitation to rejoin them before the war began and to learn their new game was utterly unexpected. I think it was entirely due to meeting Ronnie and showing him, a little, how a pair of skis should be used to enable one to enjoy the snow.[1]

I spent a lot of my time on skis after my return from Africa. Several of my cousins skied regularly every winter, and I joined them. They introduced me to the Arlberg and to their friends in St Anton, and these nice folk took me into the mountains and taught me how to enjoy them. Then I went with my father to Mürren, at Arnold Lunn's invitation. My uncle Teddy and my aunt Norah were there, invited by Arnold because of Uncle's reputation as the father of British skiing and because my aunt was an old school-friend of the Queen of Sweden. She and the King used to go to Mürren *incognito* because he liked skiing, and Arnold looked after them very carefully. So this could work, although most members of the 'K' Club knew who they were.

A word about the 'K': the Kandahar Club was a racing club started by Arnold.[2] He collected some of the best of the young British skiers, and got them trained to a point where they could beat the Swiss or the Austrians in a downhill race. That must have been around 1920, when the whole idea of downhill straight racing was started by us. By 1930, our men, although still good, could not hope to beat the Swiss or the Austrians. Yet Billy Bracken, who had trained our racers in the '20s, was still in 1930 regarded as one of the best and fastest skiers, who had won both downhill and slalom against

Colonel J. R. Macdonell DSO,
Queen's Ninth Royal Lancers
(1899–1944).

all comers at St Anton.[3] Billy was still running the racing training at Mürren in 1930. We became close friends, and I profited by skiing with him for many years after. I was not an expert. I could go straight and hold it, and I used very long skis in those days, but I had the background, so I picked up technique quickly; by the end of those first few weeks at Mürren, I had managed to be placed second in an open slalom and had won an open downhill. So they gave me a gold 'K' and invited me back. The next year, as I still had no job, I spent a couple of months at Mürren, being able to put up at a very cheap, but quite comfortable hotel because I was a 'K' member. The Mürren hotels made special rates for us because we brought other customers.

This was my first introduction to the inside of the skiing racket. At the end of the 1931 season, I went over to Davos and had a crack at the Parsenn Derby. Two years later, I had another go at that remarkable race. It is from the Parsenn Furka to Küblis, and the record then was under fifteen minutes.[4] I managed to do it in under twenty and was given a bronze ski as third in my class (those over thirty). I managed it without falling, too, which gave me quite a kick. That year, I was helping Billy, who had left Mürren and set up a club called the Gadarene at Davos. This enabled Bill to continue to teach. The Swiss would not at that date allow a foreigner to acquire a Swiss ski-teacher's licence, but you could do what you liked if you ran a racing club. I acted as general whipper-in for Billy for two seasons.

'K'-itis

Swiftly the Bubbles rise and swiftly fall
the Carefree Songsters cry their yodels long.
Thoughout the Oberland is heard the call
of the Elect (the owners of it all!)
— This is their Song —

1. WE are the 'K'
    Silver or gold we bear.
   WE are the 'K'
    Go ye in fear
    — oh Neophites!
   Lest, by the nervous way
   ye wield your 'boards', ye may
   Cause us to jeer
    — Ye Lone-tru-itis!

2. 'Alpha' and 'Ace'+

3. Awful our fate!
   WE of the Silver Guard.
   Fearful our rate,
    Soft snow or hard,
     we dare not falter!
   Kick-turn we never may
    lest some Supremer 'K'
    Become irate –
     And fetch a halter

4. "Scratch not, nor Neat!"

Above: Illustration of 'K'-itis poem. See Appendix V.

Right: Illustration of 'K'-itis poem, possibly of Arnold Lunn.

After 1931, I got the run of my teeth at one of the good hotels, starting with Grindelwald in 1931–2, at the Bear. These jobs were as Ski Club of Great Britain representative, and I was a judge for first class tests. Later (1932–3), I went to Wengen, where I was the rep. and also helped to run (and later ran) the DHO (Down Hill Only) racing club there, the Kandahar's 'hated rival'. Of course, most of our better racers belonged to both clubs. Although the variety and length of the runs at Davos were better, I came to like Wengen as a place. It was a friendly little resort, and it was a real sun-trap. Despite that, one could get some very good skiing. The Swiss in the Bernese Oberland are nice, friendly people and very easy to get on with. The scenery is magnificent. So I was always very happy to go back there.

The tests run by the SCGB were very useful for enabling people to know the standard of skiing of newcomers. It was essential to know this before one took them out on expeditions because otherwise one might be asking too much of a chap. The Ski Club system of tests was, and still is, an extremely good one. In those days, there was very much less downhill running on the pistes. Prepared ski runs were already coming in, but they were only made by the first runners going down the same places. They therefore tended to be the usual beginners' runs, or else racecourses. To go off the piste was quite usual. Powder-snow skiing was accepted as real skiing, and ski touring in the high mountains was what the majority of skiers intended to do at some time, although not all of them succeeded in finding the necessary time to do it. A few days up in the mountain huts was a glorious experience, and skiing on glaciers in untracked

Jack at Grindelwald, timing a ski race. Postcard to his mother dated 13 January 1932: 'This is what I have to do—still life isn't so bad on the whole.'

Jack instructing at Wengen. Postcard to his father dated 17 January 1933: 'Here you see the "Swiss giant" together with one Comdr. Gossage and two "winnets" ... Just off to take some awful stiffs out and kill em.'

Ski group with Jack (far right), Eileen Allan (second from left), and others.

snow, or down through the woods below, was to my mind, and I think to most people's minds, what skiing was really for.

One of the most interesting people I met at that time (in 1932) was 'Stuffy' Dowding.[5] Later, Air Chief Marshal Dowding became head of Fighter Command at the start of the war. He was in Grindelwald with his son, a small boy then. Stuffy was a fine skier, old-fashioned British first class, and there were no English there that winter of anything like his standard. Somebody hinted to me that I should try to look after him. As the British rep., I was able to meet him and ask if he was willing to do any judging of ski tests; we had a short run together. He then invited me to climb a mountain behind Grindelwald with him, to which I agreed. Climbing with Stuffy was an interesting experience. At ordinary levels, his nickname described him fairly enough. He was not communicative, but above 9,000 feet, he became quite a different person—talkative and a very likeable human being. He asked what I did, and I told him what I intended to do about the Autogiro. He warned me against it; he thought it was not a practical flying machine and that I would be wasting my time. This was my first experience of the regular RAF opinion. Gyroplanes were too slow; helicopters were not possible.

I never met Stuffy again, but when I was in France in 1940, I had reason to have some hard feelings about the lack of any fighter co-operation to protect us from the Nazi dive-bombers. That, however, was due to ignorance. If Stuffy had allowed his fighters to attempt to protect us, he would have lost too many of them, and the result of the Battle of Britain would have been very different. It would have been playing into Göring's hands. Later, too, I had to lecture to army staffs about dive-bombing, on the theme that it was already obsolete, far too inaccurate. Maybe it was, but it was very alarming.

When Nicky's mother and I married in 1936, we went to Austria at the end of November to see the first snow fall in Kitzbühel. We had intended to spend the winter in Austria, but we received a very warm invitation to come and do a double job in Wengen. Eileen was an excellent and very fast skier. Like me she held a Swiss racing class certificate, without which you could not be accepted for entry to the top-class roles.[6] We both enjoyed that winter at Wengen and repeated it in 1937–8.

It was then that I met Ronnie at the Scheidegg. He was with another younger Ninth Lancer. They both could ski moderately and safely, i.e. about English second class, but slowly. They told me that all their skiing had been on piste, so I went down to Grindelwald with them to see how they ran and then took them down again, but well away from any piste. They floundered a bit, but enjoyed it, so we did a few more runs together, and they got the hang of my soft snow technique, which was modified 'Arlberg' for their benefit, as being safe and easy to learn. They enjoyed it and invited me to come to the next regimental dinner. There the talk was all of the certainly coming war. They said that their light

Above left: Eileen Allan (1930).

Above right: Eileen Allan in a slalom race.

Eileen Allan on a ski tour in Switzerland.

tanks were already obsolete, with very poor armour compared to the German, while the heavy German tank was now quite a fast runner and could cover long distances without breakdown. 'If they don't buck up and re-equip us we won't get away with it.' No one seemed to be very worried by this cheerful forecast, and I was cordially invited to return to the regiment. It might well be possible to do so before war was declared. 'It won't take you so long to get used to a tank!'

That kind of invitation, given after several rounds of very good port, was quite irresistible. I requested the powers to re-commission me in the reserve and in April 1939 received an invitation to rejoin my old gang, for retraining as a subaltern, without pay until war should be declared. So, in May, I was back in the Army.

I never had much faith in the comfortable predictions of our socialist politicians, that the German nation was a collection of peaceful, china-pipe-smoking, beer-loving, music-loving, sweet natures. I saw too much of the other side of that coin, and I am afraid that I did not disbelieve the occasional Jewish horror story. During those seven or eight years before 1940, I was meeting too many samples of Nazi youth. Aviation, particularly experimental aviation, was a fine introduction. The Autogiro was so ill-known and so interesting. Ski-racing had leapt into enormous popularity in Central Europe since the end of the 1920s. Already, it had a press following coming within the range of football. It was well known that Hitler would encourage any youngster who looked likely to become an ace at that sport. Suitable jobs could be found, or made, to keep such fortunates in the snow all the year. So one was meeting the young Nazis being forged into Hitler's finest weapon. They were, mostly, quite pleasant, friendly chaps, easy enough to get along with, so long as the demon of political thinking was left to sleep. Yet once he was aroused, a wild look could come, and reason tended to depart. The girls helped, with very good will. It was all too easy and, of course, extremely successful. Some older people were left to shake heads, but soon that became dangerous.

The Nazi Youth was told that to kill your political adversary was the easiest and best sort of argument. They were given a knife, to be used if so instructed, and those knives were used. Walking into Austria was a simple matter, so many of the young men there had been caught by the Nazi idea—many, perhaps most, of the good young mountaineers of Innsbruck, for example. The clever trick, which always got laughs, was to climb to an inaccessible spot on the rocks overlooking Innsbruck, and to pin a great *Hakenkreuz*, a Nazi symbol, at a point unreachable by other climbers. Of course, this kind of thing was very great fun. There were a great many Jewish people in Austria, particularly in Vienna, and baiting them was also considered to be fun.

Early in 1939, Eileen and I were in Megève, a place we liked very much because the runs were interesting, the place itself charming, and we were quite unknown there. There were very few English there then. We were interested too in the new technique introduced by Émile Allais, who had a school there.

This was started by an acquaintance of ours, whose father owned the *Paris Match*, a very popular French newspaper at that time. The Allais technique was a modification of the old Christiania turn without the 'stem' to start it, which the Arlberg School had made popular. Bindings had become much firmer during the past few years, giving a far better edging control than one had in earlier days. The specialist ski boot had not yet arrived. That came some twenty or more years later.

Our quiet retirement was rudely interrupted by a telephone call from Arnold Lunn. His father had just died and he must be absent during the week of the Arlberg–Kandahar races, to be held that year at Mürren.[7] Arnold was always president of that meeting when it was in Mürren (in alternate years with St Anton). Would I come over and take his place? This was not an invitation one could refuse, so we found ourselves in Mürren. I was surprised by this because there were several people, no longer racing, who had a far better racing history than I, but it may have been easier to bring in someone from outside. Anyway, there I was, president of the A–K race meeting, for better or worse. The job involved little, as the 'K' organisation was excellent. My main chore was to make the speech after dinner on the final night, when the prizes were given. That speech had become, traditionally, an Arnold Lunn *tour de force*, in several languages, and all equally—of course, deliberately—mispronounced. Arny was a past master at that. I am not exactly an orator, and I thoroughly dislike getting on my hind legs, whatever the occasion. However, I managed it more or less acceptably, even if the laughs were fewer than usual. Having introduced the lady who was handing out the prizes, I sat and applied myself to the champagne, which I had been avoiding before speaking. Then, just as I was beginning to feel happy and relaxed, came a message: would I please go up to room so-and-so where the French were expecting me?

The French had been the dark horses of that meeting. We (the 'K') had some ideas about them. I had learnt a lot in Megève, and it was predicted that Adolf Hitler's young men might have a tougher job than their masters predicted. To our British delight, the French, headed by Allais, had swept the board.

So, all unsuspectingly, I went up to room so-and-so, to find all the French skiers there, with a bevy of French female charm in full support, and to be greeted with the statement: 'We are hooked up by special line to the Eiffel Tower and we want you to introduce us to our friends at home. We will be on the air from the Tower in five minutes.' So it was, and so I had to do. I was so alarmed that I almost forgot my French. A largish blonde made an effort to encourage me. I did not like her scent. It was over, but the kind French sent me a record of that short speech. It has to be played on an old-fashioned gramophone with a sound box and an old-fashioned needle. We do not have one any more, thank God.[8]

A couple of months later, I was in uniform and learning to drive a tank. That was quite an experience, only just less alarming.

War in France (May–June 1940)

As soon as war had been declared, the regiment received orders to move up to Norfolk.[1] Two lists went up on the board: those officers, by squadron, who would parade to go, and those officers who would remain at the depot in Tidworth. My name was not on either list. I never discovered how this happened.

However, having (so I reckoned) no orders, I packed a bag and asked for a couple of days leave, then drove up to Norfolk in my own motor. Arrived at our destination, I found the fellow subaltern who had been sent up ahead to arrange our billets. As I guessed, he was only too delighted to get some help, especially from an older man, and he asked no questions. So when the regiment had dug itself in, I made my quiet appearance at the mess.

It was shortly after that rather odd episode that I was, unexpectedly so far as I was concerned, promoted to captain. It was explained later (but I never quite believed this) that my presence as an extra was so useful, as I could do all the really dirty work, like replacing all the equipment that the squadron had lost on its last manoeuvres. It was not I who, in reality, worked that miracle, but our squadron quartermaster sergeant, who knew where everything could be got and was a marvel at inventing good excuses for the losses. Yet he, no doubt, needed an officer to back him up, and preferably an older man who was also, if necessary, a good liar. Anyway, it suddenly became lawful for a cavalry squadron to possess a squadron captain who was not necessarily the second in command. So, it was as second captain that I went to France in May 1940. My commanding officer was Ronnie Macdonell, my old Sandhurst friend, with whom I got on extremely well.

I have read very little history that mentions the First Armoured Division's hopeless effort to stem Rommel's quite unstoppable advance to the French coast. That must go down as one of the most successful breakthroughs ever made in any war; it was unbeatable because Rommel's tanks moved so fast.

Christening of Nicholas Richardson. This shows my father, mother, and uncle Alex celebrating after the event, which took place at Lytchett Minster Church in Dorset on 9 May 1940. A few days later, both my father and uncle were fighting in France. My uncle was taken prisoner after Calais fell on 26 May.

The sending of the First Armoured Division, less its infantry and without its artillery, to fight at all in France, was a wildly foolish mistake by someone at the top. I have no idea as to how it happened, but it did. An armoured division, at that date, consisted of a brigade of tanks, backed up by a brigade of mobile infantry with its own artillery to support it. An attack by the tanks had to be followed up by the infantry, who would then hold the ground taken by the tanks, the latter having, of course, to be refuelled and probably re-armed, since they could carry only very limited loads of fuel and ammunition. Tanks were highly vulnerable during these operations. Artillery preparation and support was, of course, a normal essential in most attacks by armour.

However, not only were we sent to France without our artillery (and where that went to, I do not know), but without our infantry. The Rifle Brigade was our infantry support in the First Armoured Division, and the Rifle Brigade was sent to Calais. This was probably right, if nothing else was able to do that job, for the Rifle Brigade had orders to hold Calais to the last cartridge, and they did just that. Their holding Calais prevented the Germans from concentrating on stopping the evacuation of our other troops from Dunkirk. My brother-in-law, Alex Allan, was in command at Calais of the Rifle Brigade in the final phase of the battle. He got a DSO for that, but he spent the rest of the war in a prison camp.[2] The French were expected to provide the infantry and artillery support. Personally, I never saw any sign of either. As for our tanks, these were still almost all light tanks, but we had a few cruisers, at most enough to equip one troop per squadron. Some of them came straight to the ship from their makers. Yet these had no guns fitted, and the guns did not reach Cherbourg. I started out in one of those but got rid of it in exchange for a scout car. A large, blank, and un-armoured open hole just level with one's stomach is not a very reassuring thing.[3]

So, after part of a night (20–21 May) at Cherbourg—in my case spent on a billiard table in a pub at the port—we entrained and duly arrived at a point near a forest to the north-east of Rouen, on the north side of the Seine. We spent some of that night in the forest, in my case mostly asleep, for I had not been able to grab much of that except in the train. It was here that we suffered our first casualty. A subaltern in my squadron got run over by one of his own tanks, owing to fatigue and a mistaken signal; we had to be careful about showing lights. The next day, we had to zero some of our guns. An un-zeroed gun can shoot wide of the target. These were guns that had arrived directly at the docks from the factory. The job consists in finding out what their sighting errors are, after fitting in place. It was then that I acquired what is known as artillery deafness. Someone let off a high-velocity gun just behind my ear. I later became very deaf, and that was what I was informed had probably done it. I was certainly deaf enough for quite a while thereafter.

The French roads were packed with a sad traffic, every sort of vehicle, with bedding on the roof (possibly for protection) heading south. They often choked the roads. Then, there was nothing, then, aeroplanes marked with the black crosses. Then, at a clearing in the forest, the whip-crack of bullets came from across a valley.

We made contact with the Germans a little way south-west of Amiens (on 23 May). We lost some of our light tanks to well-hidden anti-tank guns, and then we were—why, we were not told—withdrawn. We then made a very lengthy night move.[4] There were no lights, of course, but you soon learn to move quite fast without them. We were on the move all night. Eventually, our brigade attacked, without infantry as I have said, and, so far as my ears could tell, without any artillery preparation.[5] The Ninth were not, on that day, in the lead. I think it was the Hussars, but the result was not a success. I saw the hillside down which that advance was made. We did advance and passed through several villages, but that hillside was strewn with broken tanks. Since we had no infantry to hold the ground, we were withdrawn. Our brigadier was getting orders, but he did not seem to be getting any kind of support. I saw that day a considerable batch of French artillery, all very fine and ready to fight. The men were there, the sergeants were there, the *sous officiers* (sergeant majors) were there. However, there was not a single officer in sight. 'They went off two days ago, we think to Paris, or wherever they live.' Yet those men were waiting and willing to fight; those men were Communist, and the officers were not.

It was an awful mess. I cannot now remember how long it was or just in what order events occurred. We were trying to break through the German advance, from the South, but without any support, because the French were too disorganised to afford it.[6] Rommel had reached the coast and the British evacuation from Dunkirk was being completed, owing to the holding of Calais 'to the last cartridge'—a most gallant affair.[7] Now south of the Seine, we were on our own. We had no tanks left capable of action. I was kept very busy all that time, how many days I cannot remember, looking for bits and pieces. In the end, I had quite a collection, all in lorries. I was then told to put our last remaining tanks—no longer fit to fight—on to a train that was meant to go to the coast, then to collect stragglers, tank drivers, etc., into lorries, and make for the extreme west of Brittany. There might be a ship at Brest. So I did that, and when we arrived at Brest, there was a ship just about to leave, and she was the last. Arriving at Brest, I was told that no vehicles could be taken on the ship, so we put them in the harbour.[8]

The ship was full of very angry Canadians. They had some excuse for anger, since they had been sent to Norway but never landed. There, too, the Nazis had moved too fast for us. Now, they had reached France, but again not to land. We had to make use of the ship's hoses to pacify them. It is quite amazing how quickly a ship's hose will quell a riot. I sympathised with them, but we needed to sleep. We woke up in Plymouth Sound.

I landed early, to get to a bank, for the men's pay. How nice and clean and friendly it all looked. Yet at the bank, people eyed me and made way for me. Perhaps I looked a bit odd. I was not, certainly, exactly clean in my battle dress, which had been slept in, for how many nights I could not say.

Hitler was talking of invasion if the British would not come to their senses and make peace, as the French were busy doing in Bordeaux. However, we were allowed to go on leave, all of us, as if there was no scare on. Maybe that was good sense, for we were a very tired bunch of chaps.

Air Liaison Officer (1940–3)

After my return to regimental duties, I was advised to try to get into Air Intelligence as a liaison officer between the Army and Air Force. I did the necessary course for air liaison, and in early autumn, I found myself with a reconnaissance squadron. They were a nice bunch of boys and the other two ALOs were pleasant chaps. One was Hamish (Jimmy) Hamilton, who had done much flying in his own aircraft. Jimmy and I got along well together, and he was married to a very charming Italian. The job of ALO is to get to know the young pilots even better than their commanding officer. One becomes a kind of uncle. This is essential so that when a young pilot (as they all were) returns from his mission, one can translate his visual impressions. What he has seen is not always what he thinks he has seen. That, and photographic interpretation, which is a most fascinating job.

I did that job with three squadrons, but the first two were the best, from my point of view, because they were still flying two-seater aircraft. So the ALO could go up in the gun-cockpit behind the pilot. This was strictly against all the rules, but it was a good thing to do and could usually be arranged. The pilots enjoyed it, as it gave them a chance to attempt to make 'uncle' airsick or to pass him out in a terminal velocity dive. ALOs were usually picked as being immune from the effects of aerobatics, but the boys tried very hard.

As I had done a lot of flying over England, I was quite useful at finding the way, and my young pilots would sometimes get themselves utterly lost. It was up to me to find the way home, which I usually managed to do. So, we got on very well. The main trouble was the drinking in the evenings. You had to drink with the boys, and they could drink a considerable amount. The worst thing was to be attached to a Polish squadron. I had one for about four months and that really was tough going. The Poles were awfully nice, but what they could do in the way of downing liquor was quite fantastic.

Well, that was ordinary air staff work. Nothing very unusual had happened so far. Yet about the middle of 1941, I was sent to Northern Ireland, to be

'JWR with Polish officers, around 1941.' According to Jack, they were the hardest drinkers (from scrapbook).

second in command of one of the new Army/Air Support Controls, with the rank of major. This outfit was of some 300 chaps, half of them from the Army and half from the Air Force. The active part of these (as distinct from drivers and cooks, etc.) were very well-qualified radio experts. The Blue part, which went to the airfields, was RAF, and the Brown were Army and went forward, generally to a Brigade HQ, in armoured cars. The middle, or Staff, part of the outfit would be in two or three ex-motor coaches located somewhere near the Corps or Army HQ. The job was to get the aircraft to the battle where they could have the most effect, and as fast as possible. After about six months, I took over command of the unit. As the whole idea was completely new and experimental, it was a most satisfying job. There were then only four such outfits in the whole British Army. The air torpedo was coming into use at that time, and that was a very fine weapon to be used against armour, which went straight through a tank, and altogether had changed the outlook considerably on the ability of armour to survive everything. There were other forms of weapon, too, that were equally nasty. Our squadrons were armed with this. We never in training used an entire squadron, only one or two aircraft, usually one, but this would enable us to know exactly how long it took for an aircraft to arrive on the scene of the battle. It worked amazingly quickly and amazingly well. We had the best available wireless equipment and picked men to use it.

At that time America came into the war (7 December 1941), and American troops arrived in large contingents in Northern Ireland. These had to be partly retrained for battle conditions—i.e. not to have to put all orders through a typewriter, etc. They were being prepared for the North African campaign. They were very nice people to work with. My job was to bring the air into every exercise. I seem to have been good at it.[1] I enjoyed this period of the war very much, but it was entirely training, and this can become a little boring.

This very specialised work brought me constantly into touch with some very senior officers, in particular with Brigadier Crawford, who was in charge of all that went on in Northern Ireland, as he was brigadier general staff for that area. For some reason, we got on well. He would often drop in at our caravan, sometimes in the early morning. He would usually find us playing chess. Bridge was an alternative, but I prefer chess myself. Crawford seemed to think chess a good way of keeping awake, and from his comments, he was a chess player himself.

Towards the spring of 1943, we were moved to England, and at about that time, Crawford became the first director air at the War Office. This was a brand-new appointment, the WO never having had a director air before. Yet the Army now had airborne troops, parachutists, glider pilots, and the very specialised flying gunners, the gunners having found it was satisfactory, for many reasons, to fly their own light aircraft for observation, rather than to be flown by the RAF. The pilot, a gunner officer, would stay low down out of

'Pilot's cockpit of Pitcairn Autogyro P-39 Scarab, December 1941.' Built by Pitcairn in partnership with Cierva, for the British Air Ministry. Only six were made. The Experimental Aircraft Association have pictures of the only surviving example of this type of plane on their website, including a virtual tour of the cockpit (from scrapbook).

enemy observation and would only bob up when the guns were about to fire. They found that method gave them far better control and far fewer casualties. So the Army now had its own aircraft. It was then that I happened to get in touch with Alan Marsh, now commanding the RAF's only Autogiro squadron, not far from Aylesbury.

They even got gyroplanes out of museums and rebuilt them. A squadron of gyroplanes was formed during the war, quite early on. At the end of the war, it had fifteen flying, and most of the officers had been taught by Marsh and myself before the war. There was at least one DFC in that outfit, but no one would really tell you what it had been given for. I think it was for picking up spies at night, but the main job of the gyroplane, for which no other aircraft was suitable, was found to be radar calibration. Its ability to maintain height at very low wind speeds enabled it to hover, or hover with a certain amount of vertical loss of height, for a sufficient length of time, over a marker. All that was necessary was that you had some marker in the sea on which to calibrate your radar, and the gyroplane went out and hovered over it, until the machine had been calibrated—a very tiresome and dull yet necessary job.[2]

Half of Alan's pilots had been trained by us at Cierva's before the war. Alan told me that events were moving fast in the USA, where there were a number of firms with safe and flyable helicopters, and that Sikorsky and some others had orders from the US Army and Navy. He also said that Brie, who had been in America since the start of the war, had recently come over to England and persuaded our Admiralty to give Sikorsky a big order.

One of the senior chaps in 'D' Air at the War Office was an old friend, with whom I had worked earlier in the war. I talked to him and found that the War Office knew nothing of these developments. So I wrote to Crawford.[3] As a result, I found myself transferred to Marsh's squadron for refresher flying. I got about five months with them (8 July–6 December), during which Alan simply handed over one of his Autogiros to me to use as I liked and to go where I liked. That was a very interesting time. I used to go down to visit the Air Support Control unit on Salisbury Plain from time to time, which was being run by my second in command.

There was an amusing little argument about my 'wings' (flying badge). Strictly speaking, I was not entitled to wear wings since I had had no training in the RAF and I was not a member of the gunner flying team, who were the only other people, with the gliders, entitled to wear them. However, I said it would be impossible for me to be in America, trying to put on a lot of 'dog' and impress the flying people, unless I was wearing a pair of wings of some kind. After a good deal of argument with the RAF it was allowed, and I was given a pair of army wings. They were, I suppose, the first army wings to be granted to a future helicopter pilot.[4]

Date	Type	No.	Pilot, or 1st Pilot	2nd Pilot, Pupil or Passenger	DUTY (Including Results and Remarks)	SINGLE-ENGINE AIRCRAFT				
						DAY		NIGHT		
						Dual (1)	Pilot (2)	Dual (3)	Pilot (4)	Dual (5)
—	—	—	—	—	— Totals Brought Forward	91·50	387·25	2·25	·45	
4	Rota C.30	DR622	F/o Harper	Self	Local dual - HALTON	·30				
"	"	"	Self	—	Local flying "		·30			
"	"	"	"	—	" "		·45			
5	"	"	"	—	" "		·45			
"	"	"	"	—	" "		·50			
"	"	"	"	—	" "		1·00			
6	"	AP507	"	—	" "		·40			
"	"	"	"	—	" "		·10	Islanded twin		
9	"	"	F/o Harper	Self	} { Local advanced dual slow flying and engine landings	1·00	·30			
"	"	"	"	"						
10	"	"	Self	—	Local flying slow & engine landings	·20				
11	"	"	F/o Harper	Self	dual landings across runways	35	·45			
"	"	"	Self	S/ldr Tedd	Local flying with passenger		·30			
12	"	"	"	—	Local flying		·35			
13	"	"	"	—	"		·30			
16	D.H. Hornet	K9389	F/lt Ansell	Self	Local dual	·30	·45			
"	Rota. C.30	AP507	Self	—	Local flying		·25			
16	" "	"	S/ldr March	Self	Front seat dual	15				
17	" "	"	Self	—	Local flying		·45			
19	" "	DR624	"	—	" "		·20			
"	" "	"	"	—	Revd and return to Halton		2·05			
23	Oxford	7238	S/ldr March	—	Local HALTON	—	—			
			GRAND TOTAL [Cols. (1) to (10)] 499 Hrs. 75 Mins.		Totals Carried Forward	96·00	401·15	2·26	·45	

From the logbook, recording Jack's refresher course, flying C.30 AP 507 (6–13 August 1943), now on display in the Science Museum.

America: Learning to Fly the Helicopter (1943–4)

Around Christmas 1943, I found myself in one of the *Queen*s, on my way to the USA. The ship was empty, and it was a very pleasant voyage, very different from coming back the other way. In New York, I was found rooms in a hotel over a main subway station, to be convenient in the morning. I was the senior officer in charge of a mixed party of about a dozen RAF and Naval pilots, all young. I was the only soldier on that party, which was the first bunch of British regular officers to be trained as helicopter pilots. This training was carried out at Floyd Bennett Field outside New York. The US Coast Guard was given the job of setting up this helicopter school. It was run with a Swede in charge—a very nice fellow. The US Coast Guard has its own air fleet, both aircraft and airships. As such a school was quite new, the procedure for training was worked out step by step as we went along, with a conference of pupils and teachers after every exercise. The technique of flying a helicopter is utterly differed from that for an aeroplane, and some of it (such as hovering) is unlike any other kind of flying and highly skilled.

There were other objects to my visit to the US. I had to attend conferences at the Pentagon, the US War Office in Washington, on the future use and first operational trials for the helicopters. I also had to put in a bid for some early machines to be sent to us for training purposes. I had to visit all those firms, some half dozen, that had various types of helicopter under development. There were many very different ideas as to the best configuration. The main problem was to counteract the torque caused by the driven rotor, which would turn the aircraft in the opposite sense to the rotor if not counteracted. Sikorsky did this with a small vertical fan at the tail. Others were using two main rotors placed either side by side or at the front and back of the helicopter. There was even a machine flying with intermeshing rotors. I flew in some of these—but never in an intermeshing one—and made a long, very detailed report, which was sent to the War Office.[1]

Right: Cover of *Life* magazine (21 June 1943): Sikorsky's helicopter. 'Our first glimpse of it despite naval order!' (from scrapbook).

Below: Life (21 June 1943), p. 81: 'Igor Ivanovitch Sikorsky looks like an oldtime aeronaut in the cockpit of his VS-300' (from scrapbook).

'The Sikorsky YR4. The first helicopter released for service use.' Floyd Bennett Field, New York (Spring 1944) (from scrapbook).

I was also offered a flight in a type of gyroplane, of which a number had been built, which was very much in advance of anything we had done just before the war. This thing did not have a vertical take-off, but it started to climb the moment it began to move forward and climbed quite steeply, even with no wind to help it. The machines were specifically built to an army requirement, for observation purposes and gunnery observation. I put in a hot recommendation that we should get them, but nothing came of it because it was helicopters or nothing. The helicopters, however, were not obtainable. I did my best, but the Americans had their own plans for using them as they came off the line. Those for the Navy were a larger version of the existing machine, and although several of them had been built and were on trials, none of them were yet being delivered. In fact, I do not think any were delivered until after the war.[2] So that part of my mission did not succeed. There was nothing that could be done about it. The Americans, however, were extremely helpful. The flying course was excellently run, and I got a very good insight into the problems that beset the helicopter and its pilot.

I was passed out as a fully trained helicopter pilot on 11 April 1944, the first and only pilot to be so trained in the British Army.[3] I held that very useful position for about a year after my return to the UK in April 1944. It, of course, gave me many unique advantages.

My stay in the USA was most interesting, and in my rare spare time I had a lot of fun. Mostly I was in New York, but I got as far as Washington to the south and Wright Field to the west. Wright Field is a testing ground rather similar to our Farnborough. I found the US Coast Guard pilots a very nice bunch. They were mostly second-generation Americans, which meant that they had a great similarity one to another, all 100 per cent US citizens. However, their families, mostly living in or near New York, were often 100 per

Right: Sikorsky YR4 helicopters (from scrapbook).

Below: 'The first helicopter school at Floyd Bennett Field, Brooklyn, N.Y. (6 March 1944)' (from scrapbook).

XR-5 SER. NO. 43-28236 REBUILT. LOAD CARRYING -
TOTAL OF 10 PERSONS   3-25-44

XR-5 Twelve up!

Sikorsky XR-5 carrying loads of ten or twelve people, at Bridgeport, USA (March 1944), and XR-5 with capsule (from scrapbook).

cent whatever nationality they had been on arrival in the USA, more Nordic than the Norwegians, more Slav than the Slavs.

I had an amusing experience one evening. The airfield (Floyd Bennett) was at an extremity of the subway. At the entry to the station was a gate arrangement with a small pillbox office, inhabited by an elderly, fierce-looking female, who dished out change and prevented kids from getting through the turnstile without payment. This dame had a good stare at my uniform, then asked if I was British. She then asked if I was in a hurry, and on being told 'No' opened a door at the side of her kiosk and invited me in for a cup of coffee.

Of course, I accepted, and I sat in there for about an hour. The lady came from Yorkshire, where I had been fairly recently, and she proved most interesting. She had been in the subways for some twenty years and was married, with grown-up children, both in good jobs. Her husband was also in the subway service, which, she told me, was a good service to be in. Her coffee was excellent. Yet can you imagine a major in uniform being invited into a similar office in the UK? Wherever I went, Americans were charming. Their hospitality was quite overwhelming and often made the task of getting on with my job quite difficult.

England (1944–54)

The ship bringing me home (the other *Queen*) in April 1944 was a very different cup of tea to that in which I had arrived. She was so packed with troops that you could not get a cat aboard. The discipline in that ship was the best I had ever seen, anywhere. I was told that 75 per cent of the troops aboard had never seen the sea before. About 50 per cent were black.

The voyage was peculiar in several ways. As a major, I rated the use of a cabin for eight hours per twenty-four, but one was better off than most people, who had to sleep on deck. There was no distinction between day and night. Two meals were served to everyone per twenty-four hours, again with no distinction: breakfast or dinner, it made no difference. Foods were served and you ate what you needed of them. There was no unoccupied space on any enclosed deck. Where men did not sleep, they played 'craps', that American dice game. In the officers' lounge, there were tables for poker. These poker sessions never stopped, except for lifeboat drills. When one chap left a table, another took his seat. I did not dare play poker on that ship. I had played with the RAF, and I knew my limitations too well. Certainly, I was not going to play in that crowd.

We never saw another ship. We moved at high speed and seemingly alone. We had our protective air escorts, no doubt, but we never saw them. The anti-submarine escorts were somewhere over the horizon, and we relied to a great extent on speed. The two *Queens* were among the fastest ships in the world. So they could avoid the German sub packs, provided it was known where these were. They got through that war, providing perhaps as many as two crossings per month of the Atlantic, bringing us material and armaments and men. They never got caught.

We arrived at the entrance to the Firth of Clyde very early one morning and came up that river in stately majesty. The upper deck was a sort of reserve, for the ship's officers of course, and for the more senior Americans, and the very

few British officers on board were also invited to use it. On that morning, it
was fairly crowded, all in groups, say ten US officers to one Englishman. The
lies that were told were phenomenal. Factories became ancient castles; there
seemed no end to invention, if facts proved too inartistic. I am afraid that I
was not altogether innocent, but what had triggered off this spate of charming
lying was the order, 'We are entering a war area: steel helmets will be worn'.
In the Clyde? Ah well, no doubt our American friends soon learnt the score.

My return was in April 1944, a short while before D-Day (6 June).
I was then a senior air liaison officer to a Wing of fighters, located at
Shorncliffe in Hampshire. The wing, so far as I remember, consisted of one
French, one Canadian, and one Belgian fighter squadron. Its job was to
provide the top cover for the whole invasion operation—an extremely nice
crowd of young men.

Some seven days, more or less, before the actual D-Day (we did not know
when exactly that would be until twenty-four hours before), I went up to a
London suburb with the commanding officer of the wing. We were carefully
vetted at the entry to the barracks and directed into a small lecture hall. This
seemed to contain no member of the audience under the rank of major. When
the doors had closed, a very senior army officer walked on to the stage and
said: 'Gentlemen, what you are about to hear, and carry away with you, is
sheer dynamite. Nobody, but nobody else, is even to know of it. Until we
give you further instructions, nobody else may see it.' After that rather
theatrical introduction, we were told, and shown on a screen, exactly how the
re-invasion of France was planned—maps and all, and, most fascinating, the
details of the covering deception plan. This was to lead the Germans to think
that what they at first saw was a fake, that the real attacks would be much
further up the Channel. This worked. There was a rather imposing dummy
walking up the Channel, with all trimmings of air escort and smoke cover,
etc., and it worked. They kept back their armour; Rommel was not allowed to
move his reserves of tanks, until it was too late.

I had to find my own way back from outer London to Shorncliffe, with
a briefcase full of these secrets, by underground and train, because my
commanding officer had to go elsewhere with the car. It was probably as safe
as any other way, but it did not feel safe. I tried not to look too hard at my
briefcase, which was in the rack above my head. I was very happy to get back
behind the gates at Shorncliffe.

D-Day, so long expected, so dreaded, was for us at Shorncliffe without
incident. Our pilots went out bravely in the expectation of great events and
nothing happened to them. So far as I can remember, they all came back,
having seen no German aircraft. The next day was the same. Nothing came up
to them. As the high cover, they were not allowed to go down unless forced to
do so in combat. Now they were begging to be allowed to do so. The fact was

that our pre-invasion bombing of the German airfields had been so successful that the Germans could not spare the fighters to come up to meet our high cover. So the high cover was abandoned, and our pilots were allowed to go down to seek an enemy. The result of this, upon the French and Belgians, was, psychologically, interesting, but for our intelligence officers rather worrying, for every other Frenchman seemed to develop some little engine trouble, which forced him to land. A drink at the local and the trouble was put right. We, the ALOs, being not directly concerned with pilot discipline, smiled, looking the other way. Somehow, it got glossed over; there were no courts-martial, but the French intelligence officers of those squadrons were very worried men. Every pilot had his escape money, quite a few francs, sewn into his jacket, but it seems that they did not pay for their drinks!

After a week or so, I was suddenly moved to Fighter Command headquarters on the coast. It looked like being a rather alarming job, but it turned out to be quite simple. Fighter Command had an ops room—a smallish theatre with a big map of the battle area and girls sitting round, like croupiers at a casino, to move the pieces, representing the troops, ours and the enemy's. As senior army representative, I had a front seat in the dress circle overlooking the map.

By that time, we had a firm grip of the situation and were only waiting until our force ashore would be great enough to enable us to break out of the invasion area. The main job of Army Intelligence was to discover the exact locations and movements of all the German armour, all their tank units. This involved the evaluation of many reports and photographs, and the requests, to the various airfields, for search, photos, etc. of particular areas; it was a guessing game. It was fairly easy once we had found their traces to track the armour. We watched one such division come up from the Mediterranean coast. It was moved by night, and heavily camouflaged, and it took some finding. We got it from air photographs. We had the best interpreters of photos. We caught it with a heavy rocket attack somewhere near Le Mans. It suffered extremely heavy casualties, and this pretty well knocked it out of use. It never recovered. It was a kind of chess game, and I like playing chess. I am afraid I had little sympathy for our victims, and derived a good deal of satisfaction from this revenge for what had occurred in 1940. I think that was probably the most useful job I did during the war.

I was enjoying Fighter Command and had hopes of getting across to France once we had got on the move, since there would certainly then be set up an advanced HQ in France. Yet, with the steam of the invasion having cleared somewhat, the War Office began to think of future things, and now these were going to include helicopters. The RAF could not overlook the facts of the American development. They must get helicopters from America (already on order), they must arrange for pilot conversion, and the Army was determined to have its own helicopters. The gunners would be the first to get them, but the formation of an Army Air Corps was already in the offing. My reports had had very wide circulation. People knew what was going to be available from the USA, but we must build our own. Four firms, Bristol, Fairey, Saunders-Roe (with the Cierva Co.), and Westland (representing Sikorsky) were all designing or even already building some seven or more different designs of chopper. So around about September, I was sent to join a highly specialised group of army experts at the Ministry of Aircraft Production. The office was that of the army advisor to the director of military aircraft research and development (DMARD), the office responsible for all planning and all aircraft construction for the RAF (which included any for army purposes). The colonel in charge of the Army section of DMARD was a parachutist. He had under him experts in parachuting, gliding and light aircraft. Our presence was required at all meetings where forthcoming designs were discussed, to ensure that points were not missed out which affected the army.

I was given a table and chair and a filing cabinet. So, having no instructions, I set myself to review the whole helicopter picture, up to date, and produced a kind of bible of the subject, with illustrations and explanations. This took a few months to complete.[1] When done, it was accepted by the War Office as covering the whole subject and given a very wide circulation. I was then

'The first helicopter squadron, RAF 1945' (Andover 1945)' (from scrapbook).

'The remarkable helicopter: queuing-up for tea. The pilot of one of a number of helicopters used in an R.A.F. training course receiving his cup from a mobile canteen girl, while other machines can be seen hovering near to take their turn (21 July 1945)' (from scrapbook).

sent round to lecture to separate parts of the Army Staff. At the same time, I was able to visit all the firms designing or building helicopters in Britain. This was to ensure that the Army's needs, often very different from those of the Navy or RAF, got attention in the early design stages. We were not concerned with fighter aircraft, but we were concerned with anything that might drop a parachute, with a man on it, or weapons, or anything else. A lot of parachuting was going on by this time. There were also the glider boys.

I was in a very strong position because I was literally the only person in the British Army who had flown a helicopter, and I was the only person properly qualified so to do. We had no helicopters in England at the time. We did not get any for about a year after my return from America, but during that time, I was kept extremely busy writing and lecturing. I went around pretty well the whole of the British Army at home. The Army was naturally very interested in what was to be one of its most important future weapons, as it was not many years before the helicopter became that in fact. An extremely efficient mobile gun platform is what it has been called. Recent years have shown that this conception is no pipe dream.

When some helicopters arrived in the UK about a year later, I was given special facilities for flying them. Then, having got my hand in again, I was given authority to fly with test pilots of the firms concerned; these were Bristol, Fairey, Saunders-Roe, and Westland. Bristol had two types of machine, both designed by Raoul Haffner, who had been designing his own Autogiros with us at Hanworth before the war. Alan Marsh had again become the test pilot for the Cierva Company, which now worked as an adjunct of Saunders-Roe at Southampton. They had two types of design—one a very small one, which we called a Skeeter, the smallest possible two-seater, the other a very large one with three rotors, able to carry, we hoped, enormous quantities of heavy material or heavy guns, etc. Two of them were built. Unfortunately, that story ended in grief.

Not all these aircraft went into production because later on, the socialist government at the time decided that all the effort on helicopters should be concentrated into one firm, and the firm selected was Westland. As a result, they took over the development at Bristol, where there were several types of aircraft flying, a four-seater, a two/three-seater, and a very much larger machine known as the Flying Banana, very similar to one flown later by the American Navy, the Chinook. Various configurations were tried over here, the problem being that as you increased the size of the chopper, you had to increase the size of its rotor, and there were limits to that caused by the speed of the advancing blade. Critical speeds are reached at quite low levels. Something around 200 mph was thought to be about the limit at that time, although that has subsequently been increased somewhat.[2]

I was kept pretty busy trekking round from one firm to another. I had to get to know their test pilots and their technical people very thoroughly, and to learn exactly what they were doing. Through me, the Army kept very close tabs on this development, and this was carried out with a great many

'First Westland version of S.51 developed from Sikorsky R-5.' The WS-51 Dragonfly first flew in 1948, and was used by the Royal Navy and RAF from 1950, and also for civilian use (from scrapbook).

Piasecki HRP-1 'Rescuer', also known as 'the flying banana'. Designed by Frank Piasecki in the United States as a transport and rescue helicopter, this first went into service in 1947 (from scrapbook).

suggestions from our side of the fence. In fact, we were in a position to order pretty well what we wanted. The Navy had its own ideas and its own people. The four or five cadets who had come over to America had similar jobs to mine in the Admiralty, and there were two or three RAF types also. Together, we formed the new chopper community. Yet it was a year at least before we got any choppers. Then we got some Sikorskys of the type I had been taught to fly, enough to equip a small RAF squadron. Naturally, it consisted almost entirely of those who had been in Marsh's squadron of gyroplanes. After the end of the Japanese War, the Ministry of Aircraft Production was closed down and its work taken over by a part of the Ministry of Supply. This meant that the army representation was cut down.

There were fewer parachutists in the office. It continued to be run by a half-colonel and I continued there as an assistant, having become a 'technical officer grade one'—that is a major with technical staff pay, one of the best-paid people in the British Army. So this was a very good affair for me. I should have been demobilised at the end of the war as a reservist and in view of my age, but the Army kept me on. I remained in the Army, as a technical staff officer, for the rest of my army career. In 1952, I took over the senior job of advisor to DMARD, with the rank of lieutenant colonel (technical staff, first grade). That gets more pay than a general staff officer (first grade) and very considerably more than a lieutenant colonel normally gets, so it was very nice to have for the last two years of my army career.

The helicopter job, when the war stopped, gathered impetus very rapidly. The Army had by this time got some American machines, the second type of Sikorsky, which was a two-seater, faster, generally more useful, and more military than the one on which I had been to school. I therefore got permission to fly these as well, and a year or so after the war I was doing quite a bit of flying. However, in 1950, there was a fatal accident, which decided me to stop flying as a pilot on experimental aircraft. It was the biggest helicopter that had been built in the world at that time. This machine, of which two were built, had three rotors.[3] It was built by Saunders-Roe and was of great interest to the Army as a weight-carrier. We never got as far as discovering precisely what it would lift, but its capacity was very considerable. I was of course anxious to learn to fly this, and had started dual with Alan Marsh. Alan and I had one trip in the machine together, when I was shown how it was controlled, which seemed to be very simple and not unlike the single-rotor machines. My object was to get to know that machine very thoroughly, as I was convinced that it had enormous possibilities for the Army. Afterwards, when I was having a drink of beer with him, he told me that he disliked the machine intensely, but he could not explain why. He could put his finger on nothing wrong with her. She worked beautifully, as far as they had gone with their experimental flying, but for some reason, he did not like it.

The next day, I went on holiday, and when I was away, I heard that on that very day Alan and two others had been killed in the aircraft, one of the others being Jeep Cable, who had learnt to fly when I did, and had spent all the war in America with Reggie Brie. Jeep was one of the most experienced helicopter pilots there were anywhere. What happened precisely, I do not know. A rotor blade broke, the machine collapsed out of the air, and everyone was burnt to death, I hope dead before the machine hit the ground.

This was a considerable loss. I decided that at the age of fifty, this was a quite sufficient indication that it was about time I stopped flying as a pilot, and I therefore let my licences lapse. Of course, I went on flying as a passenger a great deal more than other people. It did not make any difference to my job later at Westland, where I should never have been flying as a company pilot. Those jobs were looked after by the company's test pilot, and the chief test pilot was the sales manager, who certainly would not have allowed me to get my finger onto anything. In fact, one of my difficulties when I joined the firm was that this liaison (London manager and sales manager) did not work out as well as it should. It was not my fault and I do not know if it was entirely the other chap's fault, but he had been chief test pilot for Westland for many years before the war and had many different types of aircraft under his hat, so to speak, a vast experience of flying, and he feared any rivals. He entirely mistook my situation. I was there entirely as a military representative, to keep in touch with the Services, but I am afraid the sales manager did not quite see it that way and thought that I might be after his job. That was a pity,

'The Air Horse Cierva W.11 helicopter.' The three-rotor Air Horse made its first flight on 7 December 1948, crashing on 13 June 1950, owing to fatigue failure of a component of the rotor hub (from scrapbook).

but that is the way things work in aviation companies; there is nothing new about it at all. I had been warned about it many years before by somebody else, who had joined one of the big aviation companies after having been an air commodore or something of that rank. He said, 'They sucked me dry and then they chucked away the skin, and that happens to anyone who has been in a Service and joins an aircraft firm'. That is probably rather unfair, but it undoubtedly would have been very much easier had I been the sole military representative with the firm.

As a reservist, I could not rate a pension, so in 1954, the War Office said it could keep me no longer. I had by then a total of eighteen years' service. The pensionable service is twenty years. The financial boys in the army can never be beaten, even by the generals. Ah well, I got a few handshakes. One of the things of which I am very proud is a letter written in April 1946, from HQ Land Forces Greece, signed by General Crawford.[4] He must have thought that, as a reservist, I would be back in civilian life any minute now, and this would be some help to me. It was extremely kind of him to think of me, particularly when he was in charge in Greece and must have been an extremely busy man. Greece at that time was suffering from red rebellion and God knows what, and his job must have been a very active and difficult one. I never made use of this letter because when I left the Army in 1954, I had already been offered a job by Westland. But it was certainly very nice to have it.

HELICOPTER ASSOCIATION OF GREAT BRITAIN

DINNER

GIVEN IN HONOUR OF

Mr. IGOR SIKORSKY

on the occasion of his address to the
Helicopter Association of Great Britain
TUESDAY, 17th JULY, 1951

MENU

•

Grape Fruit Cocktail

—o—

Le Filet de Solé Bonne Femme

—o—

Le Poulet en Cocotte Printanière
Les Haricots Verts au Beurre
Les Pommes Nouvelles Dorées

—o—

Les Framboises Rafraîchies
Le Parfait Glacé Vanille

—o—

Le Café

•

Grosvenor House   Park Lane, W.I.

Menu of a dinner given in honour of Mr. Igor Sikorsky on the occasion of his address to the Helicopter Association of Great Britain on Tuesday, 17 July 1951, at Grosvenor House, Park Lane, W1 (from scrapbook).

Signatures on menu of dinner for Igor Sikorsky (from scrapbook).

Westland, the Helicopter Association, and the Heliport (1954–62)

I left in summer 1954 and immediately joined Westland Aircraft as their London manager. Westland, being located at Yeovil, had at that time no one actually living in London directly connected with them, although one of their directors was in the House of Commons. However, he was too busy to look after their affairs.

In 1945, the Helicopter Association of Great Britain was formed, its chairman being Alan Marsh. It was to include all technicians, designers, and pilots working on helicopters. I was invited to join. In May 1948, Alan Marsh wrote to me, inviting me to take over as its hon. secretary. Another old friend, Max Stoker (who had belonged to Marsh's squadron for many years), had been doing this job, but he was now returning to South Africa. I asked the War Office if it would be all right for me to accept. The job was unpaid, and there was an experienced lady as paid secretary, so I would only have a watching brief so far as the office work went; we produced a journal. The War Office agreed with my idea that it would form a very useful link with everybody in the helicopter world, out of school as it were, so I could go ahead. After a few years, there were 400–500 of us dining together at one of the larger restaurants in London.

I did that job, unpaid of course—and it did take quite a lot of my time—until August 1957, when I became the Association's chairman. Our handing over of the Association in 1960 to form part of the Royal Aeronautical Society was my idea, and I carried it through against quite a lot of opposition. It had become rather unmanageable. There was a great deal of work required to run it. I still think it was the correct thing for us to do. My reason for so thinking so was that all British helicopter development had been put under one roof, that of Westland. They had taken out a licence to build Sikorskys and were therefore considerably far ahead of the other firms, who had their own designs. Sikorskys were not necessarily the best; in fact, I preferred some of the other designs. Yet Westland was made by the Government to acquire all the other developments. As a result, the others were suppressed within a couple of years. If the Association had continued on its own, it must have become an adjunct to Westland, since everyone would be a member of that firm. As a part (officially acknowledged as incorporated as a part) of the Society, it had free speech. The twenty-five years since incorporation have proved this beyond argument. The Society was very agreeable to taking it over, as it gave it an already working helicopter section, which has remained with it in good working order ever since. We had to get a royal consent, which was rather amusing. Obtaining this was rather a piece of old-fashioned fun.

The job of chairman of the Association took a fair amount of work and time. As London manager of Westland, I was able to direct our effort in two directions, the amalgamation with the Aeronautical Society and the attempt to obtain a heliport for London.

My position at Westland was a curious one. When I joined, I did so at the instigation of Eric Mensforth, who was chairman. Many of the helicopters were still in their original factories and being developed by their original designers. In the autumn of 1954, I went down to Yeovil, to make my number with the directorship and other officers of the company. On Waterloo station platform, I ran into my old friend, General Crawford. He had recently retired and had become colonel in chief of the Royal Engineers, a very strong position. Crawford was walking up and down the platform, so I accosted him, and we discovered that we were each going to Westland at Yeovil, to lunch there and meet the board. The general explained that he had been invited to join the board of Westland. This was an amusing situation, but it was a little annoying. As a retired half-colonel, I was in a pretty strong position, but with a general on the board, it meant I would be back in my original advisory capacity to the general. However, we had always got on very well, so that situation just had to be accepted. I told him I would be happy to write his speeches for him and so on. We had quite a hilarious trip down to Yeovil, followed by an equally hilarious lunch, meeting the board. The general, in fact, was not too terribly clued up on the technical aspect of helicopters, although he knew a great deal about them.

Before I joined Westland, I had launched a campaign, through the Association, for a helicopter airport for London. The heliport had been a great subject of controversy for many years. We tried to get various governments to build this, but they all fought shy of it. 'It would be so noisy' was the most usual excuse. At the beginning, just after the first helicopters arrived from America, there was a landing point near the great London Exhibition, which happened soon after the war on the Thames. However, it was really only a landing point for the Exhibition and was not continued.

The honorary rank of lieutenant colonel was re-granted by the War Office after I joined Westland. This was very important as I had to entertain foreign visitors and deal with our own bureaucracy, and I think Westland would have been very unhappy had my promotion not occurred. Why it occurred I have no idea. I can only guess that it was a form of reward, which the War Office was able to use. It cost them nothing because I had no pension. Perhaps that is where the joke lies, but it certainly was a most useful thing, in fact probably worth more to me than a decoration. A decoration would have been rather difficult in the case of the kind of work that I had been doing, which was not particularly dangerous and rather out of line with the ordinary work of the average army officer. What they did was extremely gratifying. It was, however, extremely unusual.

After joining Westland, I persuaded its chairman, Eric Mensforth, to support the idea that the industry should club together to build a heliport and hand it over to the Government. I produced a paper that gave an account of what was being done in America by way of helicopter airports, some of which were already in the centres of cities and running excellent communications to the airports outside. I pointed out that one in the middle of London would very rapidly cut down the time to get to London Airport. That paper was published by the Helicopter Association.[1] Eric thought very well of the idea. Westland was then a part of the group of companies owned by John Brown and Company. Lord Aberconway, their chairman, liked the idea, and a site was found in Battersea by the river, which had been a factory under the auspices of John Brown and was no longer in use.

Westland would do it, hiring a suitable engineering firm to do the job of construction of whatever went into the water. However, the general layout and set-up was left very largely to myself as London manager. As part designer of the heliport and its original father so to speak, I had to oversee its construction. This gave me a very interesting year because it involved getting acquainted with a large number of people one would otherwise never meet at all, such as the City Police, who use the Thames, and a gentleman called the Queen's chief harbourmaster. He was an ex-naval type who had authority over the whole river and estuary below the first lock. He was not only a very interesting fellow to meet, but he had the pleasant custom of inviting his acquaintances to come out in his motor boat or barge, as it was called. This was a small motor cruiser, which was often used to carry royalty on the occasions when they used the Thames. When it was at sea, which meant anywhere on the river below the first lock, the bar was open. As far as I know, he was able to obtain his liquor through the Navy, at naval rates. He was a very charming fellow, and so were the police and a number of other people with whom I had to get acquainted during that period of construction.

The Westland heliport opened on 23 April 1959. It is still in operation as the major heliport of London. Incidentally, Eric Mensforth was knighted soon after the opening of the heliport. I was given a small but very beautiful little ashtray, with an inscription thereon.

It was extremely interesting working at the Sanctuary, the headquarters of John Brown's group, because one met so many people from so many different branches of engineering. The group owned copper mines in Africa, a shipbuilding company, of course, Westland, and several other engineering firms. You never knew what you would meet at lunchtime there, and always there was somebody of interest. I was sorry when the time came to retire in 1962. My companions there were extremely pleasant. They gave me a very good send-off; it was a wonderful dinner. I have seen very little of them since because we decided to live most of our lives abroad, finally doing so altogether.

Jack sketching.

20

Retrospect:
The Pattern of My Life

As I look back at my experience, it is rather curious to see that there is a very distinct pattern in its development, right from early beginnings. As an only child, I was not very good at being at school. As a result of that, I got to Sandhurst rather earlier than I otherwise would have done. My contemporaries at Harrow only arrived about half a year later, as the crammer prepared me for the examination very much more efficiently than the school would have done. My time at Sandhurst was satisfactory because I was amenable to discipline, and I was happy there and so got on with my fellows. I was not messed around by anybody. I had a very good time there. It was very hard work but a very good time. During that time, one got used to the idea that there was no future whatever. This no future, this six months' possible life after one was commissioned, was the position that everybody held. We were quite used to it. We did not discuss it. I think it did not even worry us very much, or frighten us. It was accepted as something unavoidable, but it did cause you to live as fast as you possibly could. So when I joined the Army and the war finished without my even getting to it, I was in a curious position of being neither fish, flesh, nor fowl, belonging to a regiment that was far too expensive for me, which I should never really have joined at all. That position I was not entirely aware of at the time, but what I was aware of was that I seemed to be years older than my age. At nineteen or twenty, I felt like a grey-bearded chap of about twenty-five to thirty. No doubt anybody who survived the war would be the same, but it was partly due to having missed the war, as that left a curious blank in one's life. In other words, the object for which one had been working for the past few years had suddenly disappeared. I was not cut out to be a regular soldier. Military discipline in peacetime seemed to me to be rather nonsense. Military expense was far too heavy. I did not particularly want to join another regiment and make new friends. I did not, in fact, particularly want to stay in the peacetime army, certainly if I could not afford to do what my brother officers did.

That, as a result, I went to South Africa was probably rather more sensible than it appeared at the time, largely thanks to my father's activities in the plant world, which gave me a considerable advantage over other farmers. In South Africa, I think I can claim that what I did was, for my age, fairly exceptional. I not only owned and ran a very good orange farm, but I also helped to manage a fruit-packing shed. I was head sorter there for several years. I built myself an unusual house, a charming and very beautiful one, in a very beautiful place. As a result, I got a sale for my farm, which was in fact no better than several of the others round about, as far as the fruit was concerned. It was a good orange farm and that was that. But I got out of Africa not only with a whole skin, but also having made money after only about seven years, which at that age was not bad going at all. Unfortunately, on return to England, my marriage collapsed, but that is another story entirely.

Flying in the 1930s was a much more primitive business than it is nowadays. Light aircraft very rarely carried any radio because radio was heavy. The average pilot, unless he was a commercial one, did not want to bother to learn the technique, radio call-signs, etc. Also, there were very few stations with which you could communicate, coupled with the fact that a radio was a weight penalty. Apart from on airliners and service aircraft, a radio was rarely carried. As a result, the pilot had to rely on his own navigation entirely, getting no help from outside whatsoever. On arrival at an airport, he got few, if any, signals, the only possibility being light signals, which might tell him to land or keep away. That was the most he could be instructed to do. He therefore had to have his eyes in the back of his head because other aircraft were coming in to land from all directions. At a bigger commercial airport, this could be quite dangerous. You had to be watching everywhere. In a gyroplane, one's angle of descent could be very nearly, if not quite vertical, but one did not use this as a rule. One came in on an ordinary glide and approach, copying the approach of the ordinary aircraft. This was because gyroplanes were such rare birds that most other pilots had never even seen one and had no idea as to how it would perform. You had to keep out of everybody's way, and your job was to do so. One sometimes had some near approaches to collision, usually because airline pilots would be concentrating on the ground in front of and beneath them, to the exclusion of anything else. You had to be very careful therefore not to use too vertical an angle of approach, because that might mean that you would arrive unexpectedly on top of some other aircraft.

Equally, without radio, one had to rely entirely on one's own navigation and map-reading. This was all very well in good weather, but not so clever in bad weather, particularly winter weather in the mountains in Europe. You could get very badly lost, very easily indeed under those circumstances. One way and another, life was then, for the ordinary pilot, a simpler matter. He did not have to learn complicated radio rituals in order to be able to approach commercial airports. Nowadays, you would not be allowed into a commercial airport unless you knew the correct rituals, the correct language with which to talk to a commercial airport and receive instructions. All that, of, course is quite natural, but it takes time to learn. Our life is simpler in some ways but vastly more complicated in others.

There was one very important factor in my life at that time before the Second World War, when I was in full work with the Cierva Company. This was that I was able to arrange with the firm that I could be absent for long periods during the winter, provided I was at the end of a telephone and could be immediately available if required. So I would go to Switzerland and get myself a job skiing. I stress the importance of skiing in my life simply because if I had not spent so much time doing it, and in this way, I would never have come across my brother officers, and I would never therefore have received any invitation to a regimental dinner, and one can assume would never have been invited to return to the regiment, when the Second World War loomed. This ability to get in and train, although unpaid, for some months before the war actually broke out, was invaluable to me. It certainly would not have happened had I not been in touch with the regiment. This also enabled me not merely to train with them, but also to go to France with them, and that experience, bad though it was, proved to be extremely useful in my later army career. Without it, I would have been relegated to some probably rather depressing job with a local battalion or something similar. I very much doubt if I would ever have got on to the staff, and certainly, it would have taken very much longer. I would have got bogged down, training chaps or digging ditches somewhere.

So there was a pattern in my life, although one could not see it at that time. Not only did skiing bring me back into the orbit of my original regiment, but also it kept me very fit indeed because I skied on an average for about three months of each winter, sometimes longer. That enabled me to be fit for the rest of the year. Flying alone does not give you enough exercise, and I had no other sport. Yet three months in the snow was quite enough, and when I returned to the Army, I was surprised to find that I was just as hard and resilient as young chaps of half my age. That again undoubtedly was extremely valuable to me.

The Richardson Family

A family tree compiled by Kitty Richardson traces our direct descent from Sir John de Bruce, who was an uncle of King Robert the Bruce.[1] This connection goes back via the wife of David Richardson of Hartfield, Agnes Dunlop (1836–97). Her great-great-grandmother was Rachel Bruce, daughter of the Rev. Alexander Bruce of Garlet (1637–1704), a descendant of Sir Robert Bruce of Clackmannan (died 1405), who was a great-grandson of Sir John de Bruce. This also links us with the House of Elgin. The name Bruce has been kept in the Richardson family, being often used as a Christian name for both boys and girls.

On the Richardson side, the family can be traced back to John Richardson, who was a tenant farmer on the Sauchie estate in the parish of St Ninian, Stirlingshire, in the late seventeenth century. There are graves in the churchyard of St Ninians from 1745 to 1920 of Richardsons who must have been related in some way, and there were also Richardsons recorded as living in the Royal Burgh of Stirling from the fifteenth century.

The Jacobites besieged Stirling in January 1746 and occupied the country round. The St Ninian Kirk Session Minutes for 8 December 1745 record disapproval of 'the present unnatural rebellion', and 'the dreadful consequence it would have if it succeed'. On 1 February 1746, the powder magazine of the rebel army, lodged in the church, exploded, destroying the nave and killing a number of the inhabitants and the Highlanders.[2]

John Richardson's grandson, Thomas (1745–1836), was still a tenant farmer in St Ninians' parish until his wife's death in 1810, when he retired to Linlithgow. Yet his youngest son, James (1792–1860), must have decided that this was not the life for him, since at some point before 1812, he had moved to Edinburgh and was apprenticed to one of the largest grocers in the city, Robert Shepherd, at 43 South Bridge. In that year, when Shepherd retired, James was in charge of the sugar department and was set up as commission agent for sugar in Drummond Street. His close friend Andrew Melrose took over Shepherd's business, specialising in tea.

Meanwhile, the oldest brother of Thomas, also called James Richardson, had continued as a farmer. He had three sons, of whom the second, another James (1767–1843), went to the University of Glasgow and became a Presbyterian minister. The third, Robert (1779–1847), also went to this university and graduated at Edinburgh as a physician (1807). He then had the good fortune to become the personal physician to Charles John Gardiner, the Second Viscount Montjoy, later First Earl of Blessington, with whom he travelled around Europe. After qualifying in London as LRCP in 1815, he again became physician to the Second Earl of Belmore and made a two-year expedition with him, his wife, and others, via Italy and Greece, to Egypt and Palestine.

The results of this tour were two volumes by him recording their travels.[3] This work is over 1,000 pages long and contains very detailed descriptions of all the monuments, as well as of the countries and peoples they visited. In Cairo, they met the new ruler, Mahomet Ali, who was very welcoming and gave the expedition his support. Richardson is scathing about the inaccuracy of some of the descriptions and illustrations made by the famous French *Savants*, who had accompanied Napoleon's expedition to Egypt.

He was also able to offer medical aid to many people along the way, which greatly increased the popularity of the party. In Jerusalem, he operated on the eyes of Omar Effendi Nakib el Schereeff, curing him of trachoma. As a result, he became a favourite guest of this dignitary, known as 'the prince of the Arabs', and was even enabled by him to visit the Dome of the Rock a number of times and give a description of it, something that a non-Muslim had not previously been allowed to do. By contrast, in describing the Holy Land, he is very critical about both the Orthodox and Roman Catholic Churches, and the whole work ends with the conclusion that England is the most civilised country in the world in which to live.

Reviews of this work were mixed. The *British Critic* and *Gentleman's Magazine* were favourable, but the *London Quarterly Review* found the author 'neither so entertaining nor so instructive as might be wished'.[4] Lady Blessington, however, lent her copy to Lord Byron, who according to her called it an excellent work: 'It abounds in information, sensibly and unaffectedly conveyed, and even without Lord Blessington's praises of its author, would have me to conclude that he was enlightened, sensible, and a thoroughly good man.... He is just the sort of man I should like to have with me for Greece ...'[5] As Richardson had begun his career as physician to Lady Blessington's husband, one can see how their favour helped to win Byron's approval. Robert Richardson then settled down to a successful practice in London, and married a banker's granddaughter, Mary Esdaile.

In 1814, James Richardson, the sugar trader, married Catherine Wemyss, the daughter of an Edinburgh writer to the Signet. To begin with, around 1815–6, they lived at 11 Roxburgh Place. By coincidence, our younger son Andrew and Jemma Ross were married in the same street, on 30 April 2016, just 200 years after James and Catherine lived there.

James then entered the Glasgow sugar market in 1822, opening an office there four years later at 2 Antigua Place on the Clyde, and in 1832, the family moved to Glasgow. His second son, David, was sent out to Mauritius to represent the firm (Richardson, Johnstone and Company) in 1839, aged only twenty-two. There, in 1844, he married his first wife, Mary Ann Price, whose father was deputy commissary general for Mauritius. She died three years later, leaving one daughter, Mary-Jane. By 1852, David was back in Glasgow.

Meanwhile, as James's business prospered, he bought his first large property outside Glasgow, Ralston, in 1842, and had by then acquired his first ship (the *Fleetwood I*), one of twelve altogether owned by the company between then and 1898. He was also collaborating with Andrew Melrose in the tea trade with China. In 1846, James bought the Roxburgh Street Refinery in Greenock and, seven years later, he built a large warehouse near the docks. By 1855, he was the owner of two other large properties near Glasgow, at Gartconnel and Hartfield. He now possessed 3,689 acres of land and six ships. His sugar business had become one of the largest in Britain, trading not only with Mauritius, but also with Java, South India, the West Indies, and Brazil.

David married his second wife, Agnes Dunlop, in 1855, and they were Jack Richardson's grandparents. James died in 1860; his older son, Thomas (1815–72), and second son, David, then took charge of the business. Thomas inherited Ralston, and David Hartfield, with Gartconnel going to their youngest brother, John (born 1832). David built Hartfield House, south of Cove, on the east bank of Loch Long, in the early 1860s. This had a magnificent view across to Holy Loch and down the Clyde towards Bute.

In 1868–9, David's first daughter, Mary-Jane, kept a diary of a Mediterranean cruise with her family on their lovely fast boat, the *Selene*. This had a crew of twenty men; as well as David, his wife, Agnes, and Mary-Jane, they took with them three of their younger children; Thomas's son, James; a governess; and three servants. They left the Clyde on 25 September 1868, visiting Athens, Constantinople, Alexandria, and the Nile. In Athens, they were entertained by the officers of HMS *Prince Consort* and escorted by them on visits to the islands nearby. In Constantinople, Mary-Jane commented that it was a pity that St Sophia should be 'in the hands of such barbarians'. On the coast near Assos, they had to be armed, in case of attack. In her last entry of 19 February 1869, after being on the Nile, she wrote, 'I have never felt so sorry at leaving any place or people'.

In 1871–2, Thomas and his wife took another Mediterranean tour, but on the way back overland, Thomas was visiting his railway investments in

Hungary when he fell ill with dysentery in Budapest, dying there on 26 June 1872; he was buried in the cemetery at Pest. A memoir of him speaks of his 'straightforwardness, manliness of character, clear perception of the bearings of any point brought before him, a resolute will and integrity of purpose', and also says that he was 'kind and considerate', very much the son of his father. 'For more than twenty years he took a leading position on all questions affecting the sugar market arising out of legislation.'

David then became head of the company. The Roxburgh Refinery was rebuilt on a much larger scale in 1875. By the late 1870s, production had reached its peak, with £200,000 pounds of profit in 1877, and the turnout of sugar from the Refinery around this period was about 720–730 tons a week.

Unfortunately, however, by this time, the trade in cane sugar was beginning to be undercut by the promotion of sugar beet in Europe, which increased hugely between the late 1870s and 1890s. The price of cane sugar fell from thirty-five shillings per hundredweight in 1865 to eleven shillings in 1884. In 1887, David wrote a paper advocating government support for sugar beet growers in Britain, and also imposition of a duty on imports of sugar from other countries, unless they stopped paying bounties to their own growers. Yet it was not until 1903 that an international convention abolishing the sugar bounties was held, and only in 1912 did the government take up the issue of beet growing in Britain. By 1887, David had begun to realise his private assets to cover the firm's losses.

His oldest son, James (1861–85), was a scholar at Harrow, head of house and captain of football there, and an undergraduate at University College, Oxford. He went to Sandhurst in 1882 and joined the Fifth Lancers (Royal Irish). As a good linguist, he was sent to Russia and fell in love with the daughter of his tutor, Anastasia Danilevsky, against the will at first of both sets of parents. They were married in 1884 in Moscow, but she fell ill and had to return to her parents to be looked after, as James was sent to the Sudan in 1885 after the death of General Gordon. Here, he was killed at Suakin on 22 March, his body being lost. Anastasia seems to have died soon afterwards.

After this tragedy, the second son, David Bruce (1865–1945), who had joined the firm by then, became a partner in 1888. He tried to persuade his father to close the business, but without success. He married Marion Wilson in 1894 and left the firm in that year. David senior died in 1896, and the firm was then wound up. The huge Refinery was sold in 1899, and almost completely demolished by 1910. On his death, the *Standard* wrote: 'he and his brother … were for many years head of the sugar trade in Scotland. David was known on the Change as the Sugar King of Scotland.'

The land at Gartconnel in Dunbartonshire (now in Bearsden, north-west of Glasgow) was gradually sold by David's youngest son, John; a Roman Catholic seminary, Notre Dame Training College, was built on part of it, founded in 1894. Renamed St Andrew's College, it was visited by Pope John Paul II on 1 June 1982. Ralston, of which the Mansion was built in the early nineteenth century in the suburbs of Paisley, was eventually demolished in the 1930s, but the gatehouses survive, and part of it is built into the annex of Ralston Golf Club. *Sic transit gloria mundi.*

Apart from David senior's eldest son (James Richardson), his two older daughters, Sophia (1857–96) and Katherine (1863–85), also died early, without having any children, Sophia from a bathing accident in the year of her father's death, and Katherine a week after her stillborn child. This left David Bruce; his twin sister, Agnes Ellen (Nelly: 1865–1945); Edward Cleland (Teddy: 1870–1954); and Charles William (Bill: 1872–1940), Jack's father, all of whom have descendants.

In March 1885, David Bruce (aged about twenty) writes ingeniously to his brother, James, from the company's office: 'from this you will see that this is an off-day at the off-is, the good Mr Binnie is off's head, I mean head of the office. Why office—there's not much of fizz here'. Robert Binnie was a cousin and a partner in the firm. One has the impression that this kind of work was not really to David's taste. After inheriting his share of his father's estate, he lived for some years in Scotland, mostly in Mull, but by 1905, he and his family had moved to Paris, with winter holidays in Switzerland and summer ones in Brittany. Eventually, after a good deal of travelling, they settled in St Jean de Luz, living from 1926 in their newly built Villa Sagardien until June 1940, when they were evacuated to England.

Nelly married Selby Ormond in 1894, and their early years of married life were spent mostly abroad in Malta and India with his regiment, the Lancashire Fusiliers. They settled later at Villa Dorrea in Ciboure, the fishing port of St Jean de Luz, after the First World War. After Nelly's death, Selby married Betty Lyle. He died in 1950, and his son, Pat, sold their French house.

Teddy went to Harrow and read Law at Trinity Hall, Cambridge, but never practised. He had a first marriage to Maysie King, with whom he went around the world in 1899, but they parted after this. Meanwhile, in 1894–5, he and his brother, Bill, had learnt to ski at Holmenkollen in Norway, also becoming accomplished ski-jumpers there. In 1896, Teddy was the first foreigner to make a ski-jump at Holmenkollen. From here, they progressed to the Alps, visiting Davos for the first time in December 1901, where they were horrified to find that the snow was mostly being wasted on tobogganing. A few hardy souls, both local and from abroad, had made some ski tours there in the last part of the previous century, but this had not caught on until the two brothers arrived, bringing with them the techniques they had learnt in Norway. By 31 January 1902, the *Davos Courier*, the local English journal, could write that 'ski-ing is now coming very much to the fore', and by mid-February: 'Ski-ing is exceptionally popular this winter, a fact which is to a large extent due to the presence, skill and enthusiasm of the Messrs Richardson'. They narrowly escaped being wiped out by an avalanche on their first ski tour, but undaunted, they began to arrange races. The following winter, on 3 January 1903, they founded the Davos English Ski Club, together with the brothers Captain J. B. and E. H. Wroughton, the first British ski club in the Alps. A hundred years later, over twenty Richardson family descendants and their spouses met to celebrate the centenary at Davos and held a dinner on 6 January 2003, followed the next day by a cocktail party at the Fluela Hotel, where the Club used to hold some of its meetings.

Later in 1903, the two brothers were among the founding members of the Ski Club of Great Britain. According to an obituary notice of Teddy, 'the whole idea of starting a Club in the British Isles for the development and improvement of ski-ing was his'.[6] He was for many years its secretary, editor of the yearbook, and then president. In 1904, he wrote with two others *Ski-Running*, the first work on this subject in English, and in 1909 himself wrote and published *The Ski Runner*. He was one of the few members of the SCGB to gain the club's gold badges for both running and jumping. He won the first SCGB Championship, and in 1912, the Challenge Cup for the longest jump (73 feet 10 inches), when he was over forty. Later, he was affectionately known as the 'Father of British Skiing'. The notice of him just quoted describes him as 'manly, modest, firm and good-humoured; one, above all, who skied for the fun of it'. Teddy married Nora Eardley-Wilmot in 1908, and they skied together.

Both he and his brother, Bill, were interested in genetics. Teddy studied rabbits, Bill plants. Teddy also campaigned in the 1930s on behalf of the Jews in Germany who were the victims of Nazi genetic theories. In his later years he ran the local tennis club and died while playing tennis, aged eighty-three.

After Harrow and Trinity College, Cambridge, Bill also read law but did not practise. As a skier, he was keen on both racing and jumping, as well as touring. In Teddy's obituary of him, he says that the idea of starting the Davos club was probably Bill's, as 'he had, I think, the liveliest imagination of any of us', and 'those who used to ski with him will remember him best for the really terrific tosses he used to take and by the imperturbability with which he emerged from these ordeals'.[7]

He married Mabel Bishop in 1898. His research on genetics concentrated on strawberries, and he worked at the John Innes Horticultural Institute at Norwich from its start in 1911, under Dr William Bateson. He published several articles in the *Journal of Genetics* on this subject between 1914 and 1923, which are still cited today.[8] Owing to ill health, he did not ski much after the First World War and died, aged only sixty-eight, in 1940.[9]

The Bishop Family

Edgar Wainwright Bishop and His Family

The family tree of Edgar Wainwright Bishop (1837–1902), compiled by John Mannin Bishop, goes back on the side of his mother Amelia Mannin to the Reverend Willam Mannin (1746–83). The Mannin family crest *Dum Spiro Spero* ('While there's life there's hope') was granted to William Mannin of Downe, Kent in 1577. Edgar was the youngest of seven children.

In the 1841 Census, Edgar's father, Charles Bishop (1802–61), is described as a coal merchant, and they were living in Millbank Row, Westminster. In 1851, Edgar was living with his grandmother, Mary Bishop, at Highwood Hill (now in NW7). On 29 May 1855, he was commissioned as ensign in the Royal London Militia and resigned from this on 19 December 1857. He was serving with the West India Regiment in 1858 and is listed in 1861 as a lieutenant at Carisbrooke.

Charles Bishop bought Hendon Park, at Mill Hill, which had belonged to William Wilberforce, the reformer. Charles left it to his two surviving sons Henry and Edgar as 'tenants for life', as shown by Henry's will in 1896. Hendon Park House was a large Georgian mansion (now demolished) with extensive land.

Edgar married Sarah Kimberley in 1865, between July and September. Sarah was born on 3 February 1843, at Tickhill in Yorkshire. In the 1851 Census, she is described as the daughter of a gamekeeper and was living with her widowed mother, Dorothy, at Harworth, near Tickhill. She died on 29 March 1923.

By 1871, Edgar and Sarah were registered in the Census at 7–8 Berkeley Square in London, the address of Gunter's, and he is described as 'Confectioner and Landowner'. By 1881, they are at Highwood Hill House, with six children and four servants, and he is a 'Retired Army Officer'.

According to their daughter Vyvien (in a letter of 30 May 1964 to Molly Scott), they left this house when she was four, i.e. in 1888–9. They went back for a summer or two, and it was then sold. In 1891, they are at 79 Lancaster Gate in London, with eight daughters at home and seven servants. In the 1901 Census, his occupation is 'Caterer and private means', and they are listed as being in Brighton, at 52 Montpellier Road, with six children and no servants. This was presumably a holiday house, since Edgar is in the Electoral Registers for 1893–1903 for St George's, Hanover Square. The address in his will is 37 Warrington Crescent, Maida Hill, Middlesex, and this is where his daughter Vyvien was living when she was at the Slade. They had thirteen children.

Edith, the oldest, was born on 29 May 1863 in London. She married Dr Seymour Taylor (1851–1931). Her children were Edgar Michael (born 1897) and Edith Felicia (born 1898). She died on 8 May 1945. Edgar married Marjorie Ord on 16 November 1921, and they had Michael (born 10 September 1922) and John (born 21 May 1924). Edith's nephew, John English, remembered her in her old age 'living very grandly in the British Empire Hotel in Kensington. She always wore a toque as she was a great admirer of poor dear Queen Alexandra!'

Eva and Maude were born in London on 28 November 1865 and christened on 1 January 1866. Maude died in infancy, probably between January and March 1866. Eva died on 3 February 1906 and was buried at Petersburg (now Polokwane) in South Africa, according to the family tombstone in Mill Hill.

Harry Oswald was born on 17 June 1868, at 14 St George's Place, near Hyde Park. A very detailed inventory for this house, dated February 1879, is owned by Sue Attwood. He joined the Lancashire Fusiliers in 1888. After service in India and South Africa, he took over command of the 1st Battalion from Selby Ormond at Gallipoli on 21 April 1915. This was four days before the landing, in which (famously) 'six VCs were won before breakfast' by the regiment, but their casualties were very great. In a letter written on 2 May, Captain Talbot says 'Bishop is old guard and as cool as a cucumber under fire. Well I think we made a name for ourselves as we were the first to establish a hold on the peninsula'.[1] According to his granddaughter, Sue Attwood, this experience 'made him rather testy and difficult to live with' in later life. He married Olive Sylvester on 11 February 1905, and died between October and December 1941 in Andover.

Mabel and Dorothy were born in 1872, at Blean, Kent (possibly on 16 June). Mabel married Charles William Richardson in London (Paddington district) in July–September 1898. She died on 15 September 1955. Dorothy married Nelson Mortimer Richards in London (Paddington district) in October–December 1898. They had Arnold, James, and Elizabeth. Arnold married Joan Cloud and they had a son.

Hugh Geoffrey was born in 1874, at Thanet, or Margate, Kent (possibly on 19 December). He married Winifred Campbell, and they had Gillian and Betty. He worked in Africa and died in 1912.

Darell Winn was born in 1876, at Hendon (possibly on 8 January). He married May Sephton, according to the family tree belonging to John English, and they had Edgar and Doris. If the story in Jack's memoirs of a French wife is correct, this must have been a second marriage.

Sybil M. (or Sybille M. G.) is most probably the Sybil Madeline G. listed as born in 1879 at Hendon. The figure for her age in the 1891 Census should be eleven, and this fits with the 1901 Census, where she is twenty-one. In the 1881 Census, 'Typhe M.' should probably be Sybil, aged one. She was unmarried.

Ethel Gladys Mary (Gladys) was born in 1882 in London (possibly on 4 February). She married Cecil R. English, who was from Kimberley in South Africa. Their children were Antony, Daniel, Patience, Philip, and John.

Constance Cecil and Vyvien Chester were born on 21 June 1884 at Hendon. Constance was not married, but had a son (who died during the Second World War), according to Vyvien's granddaughters. In 1964, she was living at 67 Eccleston Square Mews, SW1, according to Vyvien.

Vyvien (originally named Vyvian) married Charles Henry Hart-Davis on 30 November 1908, in Funchal, Madeira, and died on 28 June 1976 at Taunton Deane, Somerset. See Appendix III.

Sydney Marion (perhaps Mannin) was born in 1885–6, at Mill Hill. She married James Mitchell, and they had Hector, Diana, and Hugh.

Henry Mannin Bishop (1831–1904)

He was born on 15 October 1831, the fifth child of Charles and Amelia. He married Helen Bridget Bond (13 August 1840–15 September 1889), probably around 1863, and they had nine children. In 1871, he was living at 38 Highwood Hill and described as a confectioner. In 1881, he was at 66 Hendon Park House, with his wife and his nine children, plus a staff of seven. In 1891, he was at 102 Hendon Park House, a widower, and described as 'Farrier' (more probably farmer, one suspects). In 1901, he was at 193 Hendon Park House, described as 'living on own means', and still with six grown-up children and four servants at home.

In his will of 1896, he says of the land at Hendon Park, and other properties jointly owned with Edgar, that no account had been taken by them of the rents and profits of these, and his trustees (his sons Charles and Edgar) should settle all the issues arising from this. He died on 16 January 1904. His estate was valued at £8,460.9.6. Hendon Park was sold at auction on 10 May 1904, with 192 acres of land.

Vyvien Hart-Davis and Molly Scott on the Family

Vyvien wrote to Molly on 31 May 1964 about their life at Highwood. She says that she was only four when they left their house there (in 1888–9):

> [Edgar's family were] all crammed into what was called The Cottage, Highwood. It was really a house and had a lovely garden, but we were such a big family we filled it to overflowing, and Harry, your father, Hugh and Darell had rooms over the stables. There was a big home farm I think of about 800 acres. Harry I think adored it all as he must have had some good times there with the horses, though I think they were mostly Uncle Henry's.

Owing to the Bishops' expenditure, 'the whole place was mortgaged bit by bit and then had to go'.

In another letter to Sue Attwood from Molly (30 August 1993), Molly quotes a letter to her from Vyvien written in 1975 about her family's artistic talents, with comments in square brackets by Molly:

> An in-and-out collection of artistic and non-artistics, Papa very good [studied at Julien's in Paris & the RA School], Mama completely non. Harry, your father, a wonderful caricaturist [he was better than caricaturist], Edith & Eva non. Mabel brilliant [she did that charming portrait of Mummy in a beautiful feathered hat at Glebe Place]. Hugh and David and Dolly non. Gladys non. Sybil non. Connie like your father. I had lots of promise Tonks told me [famous head of the Slade, Mabel, Connie and Vyvien were all there, tall blonde goddesses, painted by Tonks and I believe John], but got enveloped in designing clothes [some for the stage] to buy bread & butter. Sydney non. Well, that's the older generation. My youngest son, Hugh, drew awfully well as a schoolboy but since then dropped it all. You of course are brilliant and so hardworking. Your little mother was good at seeing you got all the backing & help available. How lovely David being so successful. I can't say my mother helped much but once we grew up Tonks & his crew came into action. I knew both the Rothensteins well, & we lived in & out of each other's sordid studios quite respectably, not as now, & a host of others, never had a penny but enjoyed life to the full. Katherine Bruce [sculptor] Peter Scott's mother was a great friend of mine, older a bit, it was she who stopped me sitting for John, he was certainly a bit much.

Molly adds:

> Aunt Connie was the one who took a job as a governess to the children of a Russian (Georgian) Prince when the family lost all their money. Before that they were certainly comfortably off, if not rich, with a London house in St. George's

Place, near Hyde Park Corner. Here Daddy [Harry] was born, & a huge one in Lancaster Gate, where Gladstone came to look at it & said the carpet (which we had later in the dining room at Moor Cottage) was too bright! It was, I think, a very nice Axminster with attractive border & good design not bright at all (but perhaps faded by then!!). And a house Highwood, in Herts, they had the sort of Dower House I think & the Bishop family were considered grand! I think they must have been rich, because they hunted 'all the time, & thought of nothing else', that would be Uncle Henry's family, who stopped the railway coming through his land & it never has to this day, leaving that part of now suburbia almost, quite rural ... Daddy's family were ... attractive, some very beautiful. Uncle Hugh was ravishing, blond & tall, only seen in photographs because he was sent to I think Africa and died there in some job, so sad, his mother's favourite. Daddy had gone into the Lancs. Fusiliers before the crash, & was I think in India when his beloved father (who used to take him as a little boy to Paris to see the ...

The rest of the letter is unfortunately missing, but presumably Molly is referring to the time of Edgar's death here.

Gunter's

Gunter's Tea Shop was started in 1757 as the Pot and Pineapple by Domenico Negri, at 7–8 Berkeley Square, selling French and Italian sweetmeats. James Gunter joined him in 1777 and took over as owner in 1799. It continued in his family until the middle of the nineteenth century, when it was bought by the Bishop family, according to Henry's descendant, John Bishop. Henry and Edgar Bishop ran the business in the late nineteenth century. Henry's son, Charles (1866–1927), inherited the firm. Charles married Anna Maria Caple, who was working for Gunter's. On his death, his son, Colin (1903–80), took over. He then sold the business to some Frenchmen and carried on as general manager until 1937–8, when he bought it back, as war loomed. Around this time, it moved to Curzon Street/Stanhope Gate. John, his son (born 1938), worked as a porter there before doing National Service, and later as a clerk. It was sold to the Mayfair Catering Company in 1962, when it went into liquidation and paid its creditors 16/8*d* in the pound.

It was very fashionable in the nineteenth century, especially for ices and sorbets. It is said to have been the only place where a lady could be seen eating alone with a gentleman who was not a relative, without harming her reputation. 'It was the fashion in the season for ladies in their open carriages to draw up by the railings under the trees, criticise each others' toilets, talk scandal, and eat ices.'[2] The gentlemen stood leaning against the railings while they ate and talked.

Gunter's also catered for the Royal Family on a regular basis. Before the Queen visited Dunkeld on her Royal Progress through Scotland in 1842, 'Lord Glenlyon sent an order to Mr Gunter, the great London confectioner, to send down a TENT, provisions, fruit, plate, wines, and everything requisite for giving an entertainment'. The luncheon was 'a most *recherché* London *déjeuner*, transported to the Highlands, & much improved in its effect by the necessity of its being spread in a tent'.[3] In an appointments book owned by Sue Attwood, in 1863, they provided for the Prince of Wales' concert at Marlborough House, and in June for the Prince of Wales' Levee. In 1889, they made the cake for the wedding of Princess Louise of Wales, the granddaughter of Queen Victoria.

John Bishop adds, 'I remember taking Harold Macmillan's lunch at 10 Downing Street by taxi, as we had forgotten that regardless of what was on the menu he always insisted on a plate of cold roast beef.'

The name of Gunter's is now used by Payne and Gunter, who specialise in corporate entertainment.

'The Crash'

Edgar had lost all his money by the time he died. The notice of his will states that he left effects worth only £300 to his brother, Henry, but his estate was impounded in December 1903. A tradition relates that someone in the family came back one day from hunting, to find that the bailiffs had taken everything. The only items of value left were those he had on his person, his gold watch chain, and diamond and cat's eye tiepin. These were later made into a bracelet, which now belongs to Sue Attwood. In her memoirs, Vyvien simply says that after he died, 'there was found to be no money'. As a result, all the younger girls had to get jobs.

The Memoirs of Vyvien Hart-Davis (Personal Reminiscences, Gold Coast, Fiji, Cyprus)

Vyvien left two memoirs. The first is forty typed pages, the second fifteen. The second was probably written first and just describes her time in Cyprus. The second was written some time, possibly soon, after the Second World War. In the opening part of the first memoir, Vyvien describes her early life in England and how she met and married Charles Hart-Davis. What follows is an abbreviated version of both memoirs, with her alterations in square brackets. I have not changed her punctuation.

I was a horrid child; I suspect partly by being the twelfth, and the ninth girl, in a family of thirteen. Always feeling unwanted and never very well doesn't help to sweeten a character; nevertheless I took note of life and its possibilities from my first breath and loved it.

I was a twin. My twin sister was graced with a lovely singing voice and was very pretty with masses of fair hair, and my father adored her; he had so many to choose from, he picked out the prettiest and took them about with him. He was an artistic literary man and quite unfit to provide for an enormous family; my Mother was a very good-looking but bad-tempered woman. She and Papa didn't agree, and I don't wonder. Papa fell down in the street when I was 16. He was brought home but never recovered consciousness, and died next day.[1]

I was then at the Slade School, but as there was no money—['there was found to be no money' deleted here]—I had to get a job.[2] A friend found one for me with a theatrical dressmakers, and I worked there for six years.[3] If I hadn't been so terrified of my employer I would have enjoyed it, but she was a dragon rather like Mama with an artist husband, who couldn't sell his work, so that she had to provide for her family. I drew and drew designs for her customers, fat and thin, ugly and lovely, and did all sorts of odd jobs; made stage-jewellery and headdresses, and seldom got any praise except from customers, and they were intrigued by my designs for them, and used to ask me personally to draw something to suit them. I earned very little, not more than £1 a week, and did work for my friends to eke out a living.[4]

I lived at a big club for girls in Notting Hill, and got a room and good meals for fifteen shillings a week, and made a lot of friends there; they were mostly students and I was very happy. I had plenty of fun with Slade school students at their dances and parties; none of us had any money so we used our imagination. I met all sorts of people famous in the theatrical world and designed their clothes.

I remember Mrs. Patrick Campbell coming for her clothes for some play. She always took off all her clothes except camiknickers, which were made of *point desprit* net threaded through with blue ribbons. But she left her hat on, generally a large befeathered affair. I had to hold her horrible little dog, hairless and minute, that she took everywhere with her. She tried on everything she could find and was a great nuisance, but had tremendous personality and attraction. She used to criticise my looks to my face, which I found hard to bear, as I was desperately shy, saying I'd look much better in the clothes she had to wear as I was a big blossom of a girl and more suited to the parts she was given to play.

Others who came were as follows:

Julia Neilson, big and kind, very handsome and heavy, and all George Edwardes' lovelies, Zena Dare and her sister, and Gladys Cooper. I helped dress them all. They alternated between being very stiff with me, or calling me darling, the latter when they wanted me to design them something prettier than for their best friends. They were an absurdly petty lot of creatures....

I had a great friend whom I had met at the Slade School, and one day she came to my dressmaker to fetch me out to lunch, and had her brother with her. He was in the Colonial Service and was home from Africa. We fell in love at first sight; he was wonderful to me, and from then on till his leave came to an end I lived in a dream. He was wonderfully good-looking; black wavy hair, very blue eyes and a brown skin, he seemed perfect to me. We used to lunch daily at the Ritz, and after my humble meals at an ABC it was very different. I went up to Lancashire to stay with his parents who lived in a lovely old black and white house. I was just in heaven except at night, as the house was haunted and I've always hated the idea of ghosts. When his leave came to an end and we had to part, I was of course in floods of tears; I always cried. We planned to be married on his next leave and I went back to work....

After about five months my fiancé got a persistent fever, and was ordered to Madeira for a month. He telegraphed his sister to bring me out and to meet him at once, so that we could spend the month together....

They travelled via the Union Castle liner *Saxon*—very rough in the Bay of Biscay—in a cabin with her future sister-in-law and another woman. Vyvien unscrewed the bolts on the porthole to let in some air and was drenched. The steward put it back and ticked her off. She and one other passenger were the only ones still up, and after two days he proposed to her—probably because they both were not seasick, enjoyed the wind, and ate huge meals. On arrival, they were kept for two hours by Customs because they had a bottle of brandy and two yellow-backed novels.

They went in an ox-carriage on a sledge to Reed's Hotel. Funchal was 'so picturesque'. Charles arrived an hour later. Sightseeing together was on horseback: 'I'd never ridden before except in our stable yard with our coachman.' Peasants were very poor, women doing fine embroidery for sale.

They decided to get married, and at the end of the month had civil and church weddings. Vyvien made her own dress, a white muslin frock, scarlet shoes and stockings, and a big peasant straw hat with a wreath of white roses from the hotel garden, and a bouquet of the same flowers. 'The result looked very pretty.' She was so nervous that she had to have lots of brandy before the church—'I hardly knew what was going on.' The other hotel guests came, and the hotel laid on a lovely cake and refreshments free: 'so adorable of them'.

'I can't say I liked marriage at first and looking back feel very sorry for my husband.'

They were in the Gold Coast for nine months, at a village called Saltpond. Their new home 'was stark beyond words … it all smelt of mildew and dripped.' There were very few Europeans there. The doctor had gone mad because of a traffic accident and sat on his verandah shooting at anyone who passed. Charles had to arrange for him to be sent back home, where he died soon afterwards. Charles' work was mainly settling disputes, holding court under a large tree. He travelled inland through the jungle and forest, cutting a way through. Once, he was away for three weeks, and Vyvien visited the commissioner and his wife at Cape Castle. They made new flags for the local tribes, to replace the old ones, which had cooking pots on them, with six black people inside. To discourage them from fighting, the new ones had doves and flowers instead. The chiefs and their followers came in ceremonial dress to receive the flags. 'It was all a great success and they returned very happy.'

One day, a local priest, who had been locked up with a drunk overnight, killed him and tore him to pieces. Vyvien saw him next day, howling and dancing like a wild animal, which upset her very much.

At times I felt like I was living on another planet, the whole atmosphere of the Coast in those days was so sinister, so much fever, the English doctors doing their best with what drugs they had, but the native way of life was so very primitive, all refuse being thrown out into the open and swamps and decay all round, it was a pretty hopeless task. We took quinine every day but I got a go of fever despite that and food poisoning and nearly died. We had a new doctor by then, a really rather nasty type, he prescribed champagne and brandy for me and used to come and partake of them himself. After that I broke out in boils; Charles kept well, thank goodness. I'm afraid I've never had the slightest urge to pioneer and was a stupid young woman.

They went home on leave after nine months, and stayed with Charles' family in Lancashire. Vyvien became pregnant and Charles returned to Africa on his own. Then they were transferred to Fiji. On the voyage out, via the Suez Canal, Ceylon, and Australia, she felt very ill. Most of the journey was by P&O liner, but the last lap from Sydney was on a very dirty boat, which stank of carobs, called the *Weary Mary*. After a week, they reached Suva harbour, 'so pretty from the sea, very green, the town on a slope of a hill with red roofed bungalows and gardens. We slid in between an opening in the coral reef and came to the quay.'

They were met by the Government House landau, which smelt of mildew. All its fittings had rusted away. It was raining hard and Charles had to hold the hood together because the clips had rusted. 'We trundled up to Government House, where we were to stay at first, a most picturesque place with a garden full of flowering shrubs'. The governor was a great horticulturalist. Vyvien went straight to bed, as ordered by the local doctor; he said that otherwise the baby would be born prematurely.

The governor's ADC looked after them. It was very peaceful and comfortable, except for the millions of mosquitoes. The Fijian servants she describes as follows:

> Fine-looking men wearing white coats edged with red and sulus the same, the latter is rather like a bath-towel, they wrap it round their loins and go barefooted, they brush their hair straight up from their heads and then it's cut in a very stiff brush and well pomaded with palm oils and very strong smells. They were charming, lazy, dignified people, very childish, and didn't make good servants, so most of us had Indians.

The labour force for sugar and banana plantations was Indian, contracted for some years, and they usually stayed on and started shops or worked as servants.

They took a furnished house, owned by the bishop of Polynesia, who was away travelling round his diocese, all the Pacific islands. It was a comfortable bungalow but very over-furnished. The neighbours all came to call, 'and I felt bewildered'. After a month in the bungalow there was a terrible storm:

> We had the worst hurricane for thirty years and spent a night of pure terror; all the furies of hell let loose, and though we had hurricane shutters ... there were two inches of leaves on the floor in the morning; the noise was simply

terrific and very frightening. One felt completely helpless … We found that our kitchen had been completely blown away, it was built over the servants' room, and someone must have left a window open, so that the wind got in and lifted the kitchen clean away. We found most of it fifty yards distant in the garden of a house the other side of the road, kitchen stove, dresser, etc., and all the saucepans and crockery broken to smithereens. The houseboy, who was asleep in his room when the hurricane broke, got up and fled and never came back.

The whole house was spoilt. They stayed with the colonial secretary and his wife till it was restored and cleaned. The town was a shambles, but one piece of luck came out of it. An old bungalow with a lovely view was flattened, and the owner built a new one, which they bought.

I had my baby, a messy affair as there was no available nurse and I had to do with a midwife who ran a nursing home and came and looked after me when she could.[5] She was a clever nurse and did her best, but I didn't get on very well, and my husband wasn't very handy with a new-born baby, he found it so slippery and mostly held it by its hands and feet; after ten days I went to the nursing home and got better, and after five weeks I went home.

She had a Scotch girl as a nurse, who was very lazy and immoral, so she gave her up and looked after the baby herself, with the help of an old Indian houseboy. 'He was marvellous, very clean and with a mind like a flower', but 'he spoilt dreadfully'. All the bedding had to be dried out in the sun on the verandah daily, as it was so damp. She never let him touch the baby's food, as there was a lot of infantile dysentery and babies died. The hygiene was very poor, but one took care of one's food.

It was a happy life, we loved our home and got the garden into order, and made a tennis court and had plenty of fun. If we went out at night we took the baby in a cradle covered with a mosquito net and left him in the cloaks; most of the English women did the same.

The Fijians were charming, 'big, kind and lazy'. They lived in villages and grew food round their doors, yams, coconuts, bananas, oranges. The rivers were full of fish; they speared them at night. They were woolly and full of bones. Meat and butter were from New Zealand and kept in an ice chest. 'We bought two cows and so had our own milk'. 'Then 1914 came and there were three German battleships in the Pacific; we had a wireless mast down by the harbour and that had to be protected as it was thought the Germans might seize it'.

A volunteer force was formed, with Charles and another man in charge, as he had known military service. They had few rifles and would all have been shot if the Germans had tried to land—'mercifully they didn't and as history tells were got rid of eventually'.

In February 1915, their long leave was due. Charles decided to sell their home and join up.

> I was shattered by this as I'd got another baby by then.[6] I didn't see why he should go and fight, so many younger men didn't, but he said everyone who could ought to offer, we'd need every man to fight the Germans and might not win even then, so we sold up at great loss to ourselves and took ship for England, a perilous voyage as German submarines were in the Atlantic and one couldn't have a glimmer of light after dark. With a baby five months old it was nerve-wracking, we landed at Liverpool a week before the Lusitania was sunk.[7] The submarine was waiting around for her but thank goodness didn't think our crowded dirty slow little ship was worth sinking.

Charles got a commission as a subaltern in the East Kent Yeomanry, training at Canterbury. He had not ridden for five years:

> poor man, he suffered agonies from stiffness. I used to rub him every evening and he'd go off again next day to ride bareback round the riding school. After ten days he got hardened and all was well; but the Colonel found out he was a Greek and Turkish scholar, so he was transferred to a draft going to Gallipoli, as a staff captain; my husband hated the idea as he felt he was sidestepping his training and he'd wanted to actually fight and a staff job was cushy, but he had to go and was stationed in the *Amazon* and helped with the Gallipoli operation and withdrawal, a horrid mess, my eldest brother, a major in the Lancashire Fusiliers led the landing at V. Beach, a shambles as everyone knows.[8]

After the evacuation, Charles got home leave:

> I was then living with my mother-in-law, they had a big house near London at Bexley; a nice little village then but very near the Vickers works at Crayford, and we got the bombers over from Germany on most clear nights.
>   ... [In the house were] my mother- and father-in-law, her mother, very old, stone deaf, a granddaughter aged eight (her father, Charles' brother, was serving), myself and two little boys, two ladies' maids, one for Granny, the other for me, my little housemaid, four other servants and a gardener and boy.

She tackled the garden, and also tried working as waitress in the canteen for the munition workers. She wasn't much good at this, as she got the orders mixed up and they liked their food quick. They were 'mostly lusty Belgians'. Then she scraped plates in the kitchen, 'a filthy job, and, ye gods, what was left on them'. The workers ate the best bits, but 'we were on the lowest rations'. The women kept chickens and pigs. Her father-in-law organised the household for defence, as he had been a soldier.

> Whenever there was a raid we all had to gather in the drawing-room and we were a motley and chilly, cross crew, old Granny never realised why she should have to come down at midnight and her poor old maid, aged seventy, had an awful job to get her to do it, shouting down her ear trumpet that the Germans were coming, Granny saying I don't mind if they do, I'm too old to go on living. Nanny and I carried the children down, who were very cross and sleepy; and after a month or two, when everyone had caught cold, it was decided to let us be; it was a low-built house and we were really just as safe in our beds. Then evacuation had to be planned. Granny had a bath-chair, she was to go in that with the granddaughter on her knees, myself and my boys in a donkey-cart, the donkey pulling us and the bath-chair tied on behind, my father-in-law and the rest of the staff walking behind; thank God it never came to that.

Rationing was very severe because of the munition workers: 'In the end the milk was blue and the bread half acorns, my youngest son got glands and had to have them operated on—we were lent a flat in Brighton where we went for him to convalesce'.

Charles got bouts of fever in Salonika and was sent home on sick leave and given a light job at the War Office. They took a small house in Hampstead, 'a dear little house, very old and built like a small tower', and 'were very happy'. Charles got better and was sent to an HQ in the Midlands, and they got a house there till the war was over.

> The first I knew of it was when I went out with the boys in the morning shopping and the grocer with tears in his eyes handed me a whole pound of butter, our ration was a quarter, and burbled all over; how I rushed home, my two small sons didn't understand but I bought them two union jacks and told them to wave them, that cheered them up.

The HQ was closed and they went back to her mother-in-law. Charles was eventually discharged and given a job in Cyprus.

> He was ecstatic, he had started his colonial career there and loved the island, he had been private secretary in those days to the Governor, he thought it would be just the same and painted wonderful pictures to me of its charming picturesqueness, friendliness and cheap living.

On the way out, they stayed in Alexandria: 'a wonderful place, blinding sun, great rich houses and intensely commercial, the population had no thought of anything but money'. They landed at Famagusta, 'the most picturesque town in the world or was then'. In Nicosia, they stayed in a hotel run by an Armenian. He was very proud of his WC, but it had no water in its tank, and 'we all got upset tummies'.

The first evening, they were asked out to dinner. There had clearly been no discomfort in the war, and the people there had no idea of life in England. They were a bit ashamed of not having volunteered: 'to us both they seemed a shoddy lot'. Later, they met a different crowd, but that first night rather coloured their time there.

They rented a bungalow and furnished it at huge expense. It was very attractive, with big rooms, a verandah all round, and a garden full of citrus fruits. Vyvien had a nursery governess with her, and the children settled in to lessons and a routine. The island was very dusty, as there had been no late rains, and the dust was 'about a foot deep'. So, she had all the floors and furniture white, as the servants didn't bother to dust. They had three servants, all called Hari Lambi, a cook, gardener, and houseboy. So, they called the cook Marios, the gardener Peripoularis, and the houseboy Hari Lambi. They were a happy trio, and sang when not working, 'which was pretty often'. It was soon very hot, and the only way to keep the house cool was to shut the windows and shutters from 6 a.m. until 6 p.m. It was very airless, but bearable.

The cook went off at daybreak with two big baskets to buy food in the bazaar. He was not a very good cook, but he was honest, 'which was rare'. Food was very cheap—a leg of lamb cost five piastres and oranges six for one piastre (one piastre was worth 1.25 pence). The servants had olives, cheese, and bread, with meat once or twice a week. A big turkey cost 7/6. The houseboy got £1 a week, the cook £2, the gardener 30/-. Charles' salary was not very big, but 'we had all we wanted and kept out of debt'.

'Eoka or Enosis was going then but apart from occasional riots didn't show its ugly head.' The Turkish community was much smaller than the Cypriote but 'by far the most charming and best educated'. They soon had made many friends among them, and also with the Greeks and Armenians. 'Entertaining them was very formal but we did our share.'

> One of my Greek friends, a very rich woman, lost her husband poor soul, she dressed entirely in black crepe for six months and had her drawing room upholstered with it; it was melancholy going to see her as she always wept.

She had blinds of crepe over the windows of her little brougham:

> That was melancholy too; we were good friends though despite all. She was very proud of her house and store-room, bulging with preserves, *bihofiki* (tiny birds in pickle), walnuts in vinegar, and every sort of crystallised fruit, cheeses of goat milk and all the Cyprus wines.

These were very cheap but mostly too sweet and heady.

You could get blind on Cyprus brandy for three piastres; the people were very priest-ridden and the monasteries flourished. It all seemed to work pretty smoothly, your sins wiped out in accordance with how much you gave to the church; my husband was an ideal man for his job, as he knew both Greek and Turkish, was completely firm, and they respected him as different to themselves, as they were mostly embedded in intrigues; it was the breath of life to them, the atmosphere full of it; the heat of noon when everyone drowsed and the sun turned the whole landscape white and glinting; then the sitting outside the wine shops in the evening discussing endlessly ways and means; the peasants worked hard and lived on dates, goat's milk, cheese, barley bread and native wine and were good-humoured and content, or so it seemed. The evenings were so lovely when the setting sun turned the mountain ranges pink and a haze of pink dust lay over the plains, a flock of sheep moving slowly with a shepherd lazily driving them made a perfect picture. Strangely the shepherds wore a long length of native woven cotton exactly like a Scottish shepherd wears his plaid; the only difference being that the Cypriot wore baggy black trousers not a kilt; he sometimes pulled the cloth over his head and round his face when the dust was extreme stirred up by his flock. The latter was generally half sheep and half goats; in the spring the lambs and the kids were heaven to watch, though they seldom mixed; the lambs ran up and down their own little rocks and the kids likewise. The spring was quite wonderful, the whole island bursting into flower, they started the end of March and lasted through April into May, then it began to get hot and all wilted into dried-up sand and dust. We had anemones, tulips, narcissi, freesias, wattle and lots of others, and round Famagusta it was just a golden haze of yellow, as there was a lot of wattle planted there and fennel that grew six feet tall all along the road and the fields were full of yellow marigolds.

We remained in Nicosia and Charles became its Commissioner (1922–34), it was the biggest district in the island and he used to visit all parts of it at intervals, mostly riding; the Governor's daughter gave him a lovely mare, half arab, when she left the island. Giselle the mare was difficult to handle, the *cavasser* (Majordomo) at Government House was the only one who could saddle her up, he was a Turk. They were better with animals than the Greeks. We got a Turkish groom, and between him and Charles the mare became quite manageable and was a lovely ride. We also had a darling pony for my daughter. Charles used to go travelling round his district and take his daughter with a *zaptish* in attendance, a policeman.

They stayed in Government rest houses. They always got a tremendous welcome. The *zaptish* cooked them a meal, about six tiny eggs each, with toast, sheep's milk, butter, oranges, and native cheese.

Water was difficult, but there was a lot under the ground. Nicosia had an aqueduct round the walls and water pumps, and the villagers got water from that. They washed their houses with wet old sacks dragged over the stone floors, and cleaned the pots and pans with sand. They had a Turkish bath about twice a year. 'I think they managed very well.' All the rich Greeks had their own air pumps and so did Government House, so they could get water. They used earth closets, which were safest, and they were emptied every night by someone employed for this. 'It all worked very well.'

We went into a bigger house eventually, I didn't like it so much as our bungalow but it was allotted to the Commissioner so we had to live in it, it stood on top of a hill, a rocky one, and a garden was a difficulty. My husband got a piece of land on one side blasted out and soil brought to it and made a tiny terraced garden, absolutely divinely pretty. Cyprus had complicated laws of possession, chiefly over water and olive groves, and the lawyers flourished. It was terribly difficult to sort things out and give the peasants a fair deal, they were mostly in debt to some village lawyer, it wasn't much good trying to get it re-arranged as the peasants accepted having to pay a percentage of their small earnings to a lawyer, and I think would have felt uncomfortable if they didn't. There was absolutely no snobbery and the rich Cypriots mostly had their poor relations as servants, the grandmother doing the garden and the small nieces the housework, and they had to work hard … Withal it was a fairly prosperous, happy, immoral, dishonest community producing a wonderfully picturesque whole. We were there for fifteen years—my two sons had to go home to England to school, an awful wrench; life for children in Cyprus was wonderful, so free and lots of sunshine and both boys hated England for the first years; we kept our daughter with us and had a governess for her; the Governor's two children came and learnt with her and one or two others—we started a little school—we had plenty of room— the governess was a very sweet girl and very pretty and all was happy, though I'm afraid not very intellectual. We had three Governors during our stay there, one a very good one but he was moved on elsewhere after eighteen months in the island, it was considered an easy job and rather given to anyone who had had too much tropics, so we didn't get the best. It takes a lifetime to really understand the oriental and the Cypriote is a mixture of that and European; their outlook on most things is completely different to ours, so formal in some ways so sluttish in others, tremendous affection for their children but will do almost anything for money; but withal a great deal of childish charm and we liked them when we got to know them; my husband spoke Greek well and they respected him as they felt here was someone who would help them, make nothing out of them, and had a character completely different to their own, if he gave a promise they knew he'd carry it out, but would never promise just to please.

They were very sad when the time came for Charles to retire. They found a flat in London (20 Elvaston Place, SW7), and after three years, they retired to the country. Charles and their daughter went out later to Cyprus on a visit 'and were given a great ovation', but war came again and they had to get home on an orange boat going to Norway. In the war, Charles was chairman of the local defence committee, and all three children joined up. Their eldest son was a prisoner of the Japanese, 'and had three years of horror', but survived. Their second son joined the East African Rifles and was in Africa, and their daughter was a Wren, 'and did very well'.

> Then all was over and now the peace is almost more difficult than either world wars, some surge of evil has come uppermost and slithering its way into all communities, and one wonders where it will end, the only way to live is to do what one can in one's own small circle to help combat it.

The first memoir ends here. The second describes their time in Cyprus. A few summaries and extracts are given here.

There was a wide riverbed:

> With a meandering bridge … that does its best to follow the river, but as that often changes its course, the bridge has a hard time to catch up with it. The river comes down in a great tearing, rushing flood from the mountains once a year; it is amazing to watch a great wall of water carrying along anything in its path, goats, sheep, trees etc., and goes hurtling down to the sea. For a week or two there are great pools in the river-bed but they soon dry up and a wide stony waste is left and everyone crosses just where they fancy, and the bridge hopes it's in the right place. If not a bit is joined on and it becomes even wider.

The Turks used to bring turkeys in long baskets to the kitchen door and asked an enormous price.

> You halved it at once, at which they exclaimed in horror, so you left them, saying you didn't want a turkey. They sat on and at intervals sent messages to the cook that though they had to keep their mother and ten children, they would come down a little. After about three hours of this, they came down to your price, which you gave them with a few extra piastres baksheesh (tip) and they departed in high spirits, having thoroughly enjoyed the haggling and got more than they would in the bazaar. I learnt to bargain over most things and, when on leave in England, found myself starting it at Marshall and Snelgrove's over gloves, which didn't please the shop assistant.

The peasants were very poor. They lived on barley bread, olives, goat's milk, cheese, very little meat, and cheap wine. The colonial servants introduced a cooperative scheme, so that the poor could help each other, to keep them out of debt, but it was very slow and difficult. The land was cut up into so many ownerships, and it was terribly involved.

When they first went out there, the farmers still winnowed the corn, just as in the Bible. The chaff was thrown in the air and the corn left behind in big sieves, while the owner sat on a chair to see that none was stolen. They also used to tread out the corn on stone floors, with a donkey and a camel going round and round, often driven by the grandmother. They were so very materialistic, but life was hard unless you had money and everyone expected to work until they dropped.

Nicosia was a most marvellously picturesque town, the walls round it had big bastions, all a bit crumbled, but still intact, with gates at intervals for traffic to pass through. The streets were mostly very narrow, and the shops just holes in the houses lining them. There were different streets for most articles; all the copper pots, etc. made in one street, silver in another, pottery in another, etc. The Cypriotes were clever at copying, and could copy a well-cut suit marvellously. One chose the cloth, which came from England, and they did it very cheaply. My husband got a lot of his clothes made that way. There were also plenty of dressmakers and seamstresses, the latter came and sewed in one's house. They came at 7 a.m. and worked till 5 p.m. and one gave them their meals and 2/-. They hadn't much imagination and would practically copy a darn or a patch, but if you looked after them they were a wonderful help. I had a girl called Sussanah (Susanna?) for years, she was very fat and silent, but a nice little thing. Enosis was there but the population, on the whole, seemed very fond of the English, and when my husband travelled round the villages in his district, he always got a very warm welcome …

The Turks were the colourful ones and on feast days in their best clothes were wonderful, red fezzes decked with flowers, coloured and embroidered waistcoats and baggy trousers, the women mostly in one colour but pretty pinks were their choice. They all wore yashmaks then. I used to go to the big tea parties at Government House given for the wives of the Turkish officials, no men allowed and they let down their veils, some were gloriously pretty but they soon got fat as they eat too many sweets. They sat round the room smiling and taking everything that we handed them, but never eating it. When they'd gone the Governor's wife and I gathered up the untouched cakes and put them in tins for the household. It was rather an ordeal, so frightfully formal, but had to be gone through, as it was the only way they could be entertained.

We had the old King of the Hedjaz exiled to Cyprus.[9] He was put in my husband's charge, a fine-looking old man, he brought his favourite horses with him, and they were treated rather like pet dogs and brought in for tit-bits at the end of a meal. He used to come and take my little girl out for drives, he seemed to love her and gave her a beautiful necklace and arab dress. He lent two of his robes and swords, etc. to us for fancy dress; one was thick white silk embroidered in gold with a golden sword set in jewels, the other was cream and silver with a silver sword jewelled. The headdresses were to match, they were quite exquisite. He was very old and became senile and was then allowed to go home; two of his sons, both kings, came to fetch him.[10] Cyprus had no ambulance, so the post van was cleaned and carpeted and His Majesty laid in it to take him to the railway station, where a guard of honour of the local police force was drawn up, and the luggage van of the primitive little train cleaned and carpeted to receive him, with a local band blaring and many salutes. He was put into the train but it had difficulty in starting and after thuds and jerks got off at long last. Poor old man, he knew nothing about it and died soon after. His sons were most grateful for all the care that had been taken of their father. We were mightily relieved to be free of the responsibility as there seemed to be no income for him and our Governor unsympathetic towards spending Government money for him. He had quite a big entourage to start with, two huge black slaves to look after his beloved horses, and numerous servants, and all expecting lavish food, etc., a sheep roasted whole for a dinner party, etc. He'd brought a pet ostrich as well as the horses, a rather dilapidated cross bird that was difficult to cage, it was put in a wire enclosure and snarled at everyone, I can't think why it was brought. We also had some Assyrian Royalties exiled and put in my husband's care. They hadn't a penny, poor souls, but were easier than the Arab king as they spoke French and were more or less Europeanised. They went to Brazil eventually.[11] Then 2,000 White Russians after the Revolution, they were put in a big camp that housed Turkish prisoners during the 1914 war and was pretty primitive. The poor Russians, most of whom had never done a stroke of work with their hands, just sat and pined; a few of them tried to earn a living. One, he said he was a prince, went as kitchen boy to the English hospital, but created such havoc among the female staff he had to go, he was a wonderful horse-man and set about teaching the Matron to ride; she was very stout and bumped up and down on a small Cyprus pony, the kitchen porter cycling beside her and shouting instructions. Another Russian, I'm told a marvellous musician, but his music was so wild and noisy, it wanted a special education. He broke all the pianos he could get to play on and eventually got an offer to go to Holland and produce an opera. He came to say goodbye to us the day before he left and I asked him to stay to lunch. He ate a whole leg of mutton and drank two tumblers of the very sweet port and departed full of vim. We found the Russians were physically so much stronger than we were. They could dance all night, sleep a bit, then go on dancing, drinking and eating an incredible amount, but they had great charm and some were beautiful. They went away eventually, but as refugees it was a sad time for them, they had had so many servants they'd never learnt to do anything, not their fault. They mostly spoke French and German as well as Russian and had very good manners.

There was a summer camp on the mountain, Mt. Troodos. The Governor and Secretariat had their offices up there and small houses to live in. The rest of the

English officials could get huts allocated to them and their wives and children went up during the hot months on the plains. It was a divine place with pine trees and wonderful mountain air. We had a little brick hut of four rooms and shed outside with tents. There was an English club where one could play tennis and dance, all rather rough; and the soil being very red and the surface very stony, one's shoes had a bad time, but it was heaven for children and they all played around the huts all day. If they had a pony to ride, and most of them had, they used to ride together. Picnics were great fun, donkeys with big panniers on their sides carried the food, and sometimes a child as well, one could hire them for very little. There were lots of lovely places to picnic in, mostly with a stream or waterfall. The season was generally over at the end of September and we went back to Nicosia, which seemed terribly hot and dry, as the rains seldom came till November, and the weather took a long time working up for them. Lots of thunder and lightning in the mountains and general oppressiveness, then everything atmospheric seemed to explode and enormous drops of rain started and drenching rain poured down. The river came rushing down from the mountains like a savage hurtling wall and everyone rushed for shelter and rejoiced, the ground smelt so lovely after such a long drought and all the tension went out of the air. It remained wet for a time, then the winter came and that could be very cold with snow and bitter winds, but only for a short time, December, January, February, and woe betide visitors coming for warmth. The houses were built for heat and were impossible really to warm; we had one fireplace in the drawing room and, in those days, no electric helps, though there was electric lighting in Nicosia. We had wood fires, mostly olive tree wood that had a heavenly smell when burning. Sweeping a chimney was primitive, a man came and tied a bit of brushwood onto a brick and let it down your chimney from the roof on a cord. There wasn't any soot, of course, but burning wood rather clogged the chimney and it had to be done occasionally. Dust was our great menace. I had my floors painted white then it didn't show, otherwise, if you had dark floors, anyone coming from outside left white footmarks. The Cypriote houses all had stone floors up and down and rugs. I never saw a boarded floor in any that I went to. We got some carpets made of goat hair in wide black and white stripes, very cheap and good, for the bedrooms; and one could get furniture made in the bazaar. They were very good carpenters and copied any design you wanted.

When they had to leave, she says:

My maid did nothing but weep and weep, she had been with me all the time…I felt utterly wretched with it all and wished we had retired there, as we had thought of doing. But there were two sons in England and, as things turned out, I'm very glad we didn't stay in Cyprus.[12]

The Ormonds' House in Ciboure During the German Occupation

According to Kitty Richardson: 'the two devoted maids, Andrée and Anna, lived on in the Villa Dorrea and with some courage prevented the Germans from occupying the house.'[1]

Another relative, Chipps Bennett, describing the situation in 1946, writes as follows:

> Still nailed to the door of each room was the list…of German soldiers to whom it was allocated … However, the Basque maids had switched off the pump that pumped up water from the well to the tank in the roof and had told the soldiers that water had to be carried up the steps from Ciboure, some 200 feet below. After a few days the Germans had left in disgust, never to return.[2]

Chipps also says that the maids hid all the silver in the steeple of Ciboure church, just below the house, and covered Selby's cars in the garage with piles of logs, so that the Germans never found them. When Chipps revisited the house in 1946, everything was back in its old place, and in the drawing room was the copy of the *Illustrated London News* of May 1940, left there when Selby had fled back to England.

The version given by Pat's older son Derry Ormond, who was ten in 1946, is as follows:

> I was there in August 1946, and heard it direct from Anna and Andrée's mouths. Dorrea was occupied by seventy Bundeswehr Germans from their arrival in 1940 until they had to scamper up North in 1944 because of the landings. I saw the lists of who occupied which room still posted up. There was no furniture in the rooms because the maids had taken it all out and put it in the two garages. In doing so they completely camouflaged the two cars left behind there; my parents' Hotchkiss, and Pepe's (Selby's) Ford. The Germans only discovered them at the

moment of the flight north, but they were abandoned in Bordeaux and were recuperated. One piece of furniture was left in the house: the billiard table with a carpet underneath. Throughout the war, the occupants never discovered that there was a big rainwater tank under the billiard table; in consequence they had to go all the way down the hill past the cemetery to the public tap just above Ciboure church, and bring back all the water necessary both to drink and wash themselves. In 1946, after one lunch, the maids gallantly pulled out from under the summer house down in the garden all the things they had stolen from the Germans, including one rifle (to our shock and amazement), and the metal badge usually pinned to the peaked cap of an officer, which was given to me, and kept by me for many years before disappearing.

He adds, however, that it may be right that the Germans did leave after the 'turning off of the pump' mentioned by Chipps, and 'on reflection that does seem likely!'

Derry's younger brother Julian, who was six in 1946, recalls the maids delving under the summer house, 'to produce what I remember as a pistol'.

> I was told that the house was only occupied for a short time, as the maids did not explain that there was a second water tank, and only showed the Germans the old well just at the back of the house, which had a metal cover and pretty horrible green water in it.

He also recalls hearing that the maids had covered the cars up with firewood. The story of the escaping POWs is only mentioned by my father, and so it could be wrong.

APPENDIX V

'K'-itis

This poem about the Kandahar Club was written and illustrated by my father in pencil sometime in the 1930s. On the reverse side is the breakdown of costs of a meal, eaten by himself, Eileen (my mother), Roy (unknown), and Bill (presumably Bracken). As it includes '*schnitzel*' and '*glühwein*' it was probably lunch during a day's skiing at Mürren.

In the poem 'the Bubbles' refers to the Allmendhubel funicular (or 'Alibubble') at Mürren, which was opened in 1912, initially to service the bobsleigh run, later used by skiers. The lone tree at the end of the first stanza was a landmark on the run down from the Schilthorn. Arnold and Bill are Lunn and Bracken. To 'nest' probably refers to skiing in and out of the trees, known in off-piste skiing jargon as birds-nesting.

Swiftly the Bubbles rise and swiftly fall,
The carefree songsters cry their yodels long.
Throughout the Oberland is heard the call
Of the Elect (the owners of it all!)
—This is their song—

1. WE are the 'K',
Silver or gold we bear.
WE are the 'K',
Go ye in fear
—Oh neophytes!
Lest, by the nervous way
Ye wield your 'boards', ye may
Cause us to jeer
—Ye Lone-tree-ites!

2. 'Alpha and 'Ace'—
We are the Golden Few.
Dare ye our race
Venture to view,
—Oh, Over-rash!
Stand ye not in the way,
Lest your poor carcase may
Lessen our pace
—unwanted trash!

3. Awful our fate!
We of the Silver Guard.
Fearful our rate,
Soft snow or hard,
We dare not falter!
Kick-turn we never may,
Lest some supremer 'K'
Become irate-
And fetch a halter.

4. 'Scratch not, nor Nest!'
So runs the Royal Command.
'Ye may not rest.
While ye can stand,
Ye still must run!'
Someday, perhaps, your nation
(And Arnold's reputation!)
On you depend—
Oh breathless one.

5. 'Stem without edge.
Are we not called the Pure?'
The dizziest ledge—
Is but a lure.
THIS is our CURSE—
'Seek you the steepest hill-
We'll put our trust in Bill
For he is sure
To find a worse.'

ENVOI

As Bubble rises—so must Bubble fall!
Ah, envious novices, why do ye long
To emulate poor people, so in thrall?
Listen! The shining snows are free for all!
Such is my song.

Endnotes

Chapter 1

1. In the 1901 Census, the household consisted of a nurse, kitchenmaid, parlourmaid, cook, and housemaid.
2. Emley Farm House, in Bowlhead Green, is now a National Trust Grade II-listed farmhouse, with five bedrooms. It is described as 'largely unaltered since the nineteenth century', and still has its internal well.
3. William Bateson (1861–1926). He coined the term 'genetics' in 1905.
4. E. C. Richardson, later known as 'the Father of English Skiing'.
5. The Davos English Ski Club was the earliest British ski club in the Alps. It was founded in January 1903 by the two Richardson brothers and the brothers E. H. and J. B. Wroughton. The Ski Club of Great Britain was founded later in the same year.
6. Villa Sagardian. It is now a *centre culturel*.
7. David Richardson of Hartfield (1817–96) married first, on 21 May 1844, Mary Smallwood Price (1825–47), daughter of the deputy commissary general for Mauritius, when he was working in the sugar trade there. Their first daughter died at birth. The second, Mary-Jane (born 1846), survived, but her mother died aged twenty-one after a painful illness. Mary-Jane does not seem to have married. David returned to Scotland in 1852 and married Agnes Dunlop on 15 November 1855. See Appendix I: the Richardson family.
8. The *Selene*, launched in June 1865 and of 274 tonnage, once left the Clyde on a Tuesday and arrived in Lisbon on Saturday, in time for the opera—Richardson, *Richardsons: A Family History* (1992), p. 27.
9. He was a member of the Royal Northern Yacht Club from 1852 to around 1880, vice-commodore in the regatta of 1863, and a committee member (steward) from 1855 to 1871—Richardson, *op. cit.*, p. 26, and information from Jon Reid, Hon. Archivist, RNCYC.
10. This later belonged to James, Lord Inverclyde, whose grandfather founded the Cunard Line. It was demolished in the 1960s.
11. Mabel and her twin sister, Dorothy, were born in 1872. See Appendix II: the Bishop family.
12. Edgar William Bishop (1868–1925), son of Mabel's uncle, Henry Bishop (1831–1904). He married Louise Salaman, and they actually lived at Fifield, near Oxford, until 1924, when they moved to Fyfield Manor in Wiltshire.

13. Edgar Wainwright Bishop (1837–1902).
14. Sarah Kimberley (1843–1923) came from Yorkshire, and was the daughter of a gamekeeper.
15. 79 Lancaster Gate. They were living there at the time of the 1891 Census.
16. They married in 1905. Olive was of Huguenot descent, and 'very tiny and neat' (according to Sue Attwood).
17. Mary Winona Mannin (Molly) Bishop (1911–98). Molly had a younger brother, Harry Oswald Mannin ('Tim') Bishop (1915–86). He wrote a memoir of his life, and the part of this about his army career was published after his death, as *One Young Soldier: The Memoirs of a Cavalryman* (1993). His daughter, Susan (Sue), is married to Tom Attwood.
18. Lord George Montagu Douglas Scott (1911–99) was the youngest son of the Duke of Buccleugh and Queensberry. His sister, Alice, was the wife of the Duke of Gloucester.
19. The Second Armoured Brigade include both the Ninth Lancers, Jack's regiment, and the Tenth Hussars, that of George Scott.
20. Darell Winn Bishop, born 1876.
21. Hugh Geoffrey Bishop (1874–1912).
22. She entered in 1888–9 and attended up to 1896–7, except for 1894–5. She was also taught by Alphonse Legros. In 1890–1, she won a prize and a silver medal for painting from the antique. In 1891–2, she was awarded a Slade Fine Art scholarship for £50 per year, for three years.
23. We still have this portrait (NJR).
24. The *Revue Libre* for 1904, pp. 213–4, illustrates and praises her portrait of a young lady, 'Mlle. G.B.': '*C'est une toile excessivement décorative, qu'accentue encore le charme naturel du modèle, et la pose tout à fait heureuse.*' The review also commends two of her sculptures, a head of Doctor Dowty, and the head of a child, '*Rêveur*', which is actually of her son, aged about four. She also exhibited 'Désirée', a head of a girl. Cf. Rabutin, *La Revue Libre* (1904), pp. 213–4. We have copies of these busts (NJR).
25. Constance Bishop studied at the Slade from 1899 to 1903. In 1900–1, she was awarded a third class in fine art anatomy and a certificate in perspective, and in 1901–2, certificates in figure painting and figure drawing. Vyvien was there from 1901 to 1903.
26. According to family tradition, he was a Georgian prince, and she was made to sleep in the hall with the dogs.
27. Gladys married Cecil R. English, and they had five children.
28. Charles Hart-Davis (1874–1958) was in the Colonial Service when he met Vyvien in 1908. They were married in Madeira on 30 November that year, then went out to the Gold Coast, where he was stationed from 1906 to 1910. From then until 1915, they were in Fiji. He then joined the East Kent Yeomanry, serving as a staff captain at Gallipoli, Salonika, and at the War Office. From 1919 to 1934, they were in Nicosia, in Cyprus, where he was district commissioner from 1922. After retirement, they lived first in London, and from 1937 at The Old House, Nether Stowey in Somerset, until his death. She died in 1976. Vyvien gives a vivid account of her life and years abroad in her unpublished memoirs: Hart-Davis, *Personal Reminiscences, Gold Coast, Fiji, Cyprus* (Bodleian stamp dated 1967). See Appendix III.
29. According to Hone, *The Life of Henry Tonks* (1939), p. 70, Tonks painted a commissioned portrait group, *Gladys, Constance and Vivien, Daughters of the Late Edgar Bishop*, depicting 'three very attractive girls with lovely

complexions'. He had already portrayed the three girls in his *Return from the Ball*, showing 'a girl sitting on a sofa talking to her two sisters in their night-gowns; a big picture, he said, for him, into which he had already put a good deal of time and money' (p. 58). Both works were shown at the New English Art Club in 1902, and the portrait group was exhibited again at the Carfax Gallery in 1905, where it was the principal oil painting. The critics described it as 'a composition of three white-frocked girls in a room of many roses', 'grouped round an oval table of satin wood on which stands a vase of flowers', and 'essentially a still life study, lacking submission to light, perhaps' (pp. 325–8).

30. Sydney was the youngest of the family, born in 1885.

31. Dorothy, born in 1872, Mabel's twin, married Nelson Mortimer Richards in 1898, the same year as Mabel was married.

32. The castle was bought in 1903 by John Morgan Richards (1841–1918), a wealthy American businessman, who marketed cigarettes and patent medicines. His wife was Laura Arnold. His daughter, the writer Pearl Mary Teresa Craigie, lived in a villa nearby from 1900 to 1906, when she died. Her pen name was John Oliver Hobbes. She was very successful as a novelist and playwright. She became a Catholic in 1892. Tip (Nelson Mortimer) was a son of J. M. Richards. Cf. Marsh, *Steephill Castle, Ventnor, Isle of Wight* (1907), Richards, *Almost Fairyland* (1914), and Harding, *Air-Bird in the Water: the Life and Works of Pearl Craigie* (1996). The Richards family also owned a house at Lancaster Gate, and so were neighbours and friends of Dorothy Bishop's family: cf. Richards, *op. cit.*, p. 91.

33. It is not correct to say that Churchill was wholly to blame for the campaign; for a reassessment, cf. Bell, *Churchill and the Dardanelles* (2017). Lt-Col. H. V. Selby Ormond commanded from 4 August 1914 to 20 April 1915, when he was, according to the official record, invalided out with heart trouble. Lt-Col. H. O. Bishop commanded from 21 April to 11 June 1915, when he was wounded, and from 20 January to 13 March 1916, when he was replaced. The military landings at Gallipoli began on 25 April 1915. The Suvla Bay landing was 6–15 August 1915. The true story about Selby Ormond at Gallipoli, according to his grandson, Commander Harry ('Chipps') Selby Bennett, is that 'At the briefing before the landing my grandfather protested that it was suicide, and was promptly relieved of his command by General Hamilton, the Commander-in-Chief. It was a turning point in my grandfather's life and the end of his military career': cf. Bennett, *Seahorse! Between the Sea and the Saddle* (2005), p. 23.

34. He lived in 'an old Basque tower-like house … called Dorrea. From its terrace it had a magnificent view of the bay and of the little fishing port of St Jean de Luz.' Selby 'always used to say that Dorrea had been the command post of the Duke of Wellington in November 1813 at the Battle of the Nivelle River.' Cf. Bennett, *op. cit.*, p. 24.

35. Ormond, *The Basques and their Country* (1926).

36. See Appendix IV: the Ormonds' house in Ciboure during the German occupation.

Chapter 2

1. It may have been St Peter's Court, Broadstairs. This became fashionable when George V sent his younger sons there, including Prince Henry.

Chapter 3

1. The house was Moretons, and the housemaster was Manley Colchester Kemp (1861–1951). He had captained the Oxford cricket team and also played football and rackets for Oxford.
2. He entered Harrow in autumn 1913 and left at the end of 1914.

Chapter 4

1. He was born in 1900, the future Duke of Gloucester. He later married Alice, the sister of Molly Bishop's husband, George Scott.

Chapter 6

1. For this period, cf. Sheppard, *The Ninth Lancers 1715–1936* (1939), pp. 308–11.
2. This was Schloss Frens, in a wooded park between Bergheim and Horrem, west of Cologne. It belonged to Otto von Gymnich (1851–1931).
3. Winter and spring 1919–20 were spent at Tidworth.

Chapter 7

1. She was Olive Pakenham Mahon, of Strokestown House. She married Captain Edward Stafford-King-Harman on 1 July 1914, and he was killed on 6 November that year at Ypres. Her daughter, Lettice, was born on 10 April 1915, and they then returned to live in Strokestown. She married her second husband, Major Wilfred Stuart Hales, in December 1921. They had met when he was stationed at Strokestown with the East Yorkshire Regiment, at the same time as the Ninth Lancers. Olive died in 1981, aged eighty-seven. She can be heard reminiscing about her first wedding towards the end of a radio programme called *Voices from a Vanishing World* by Jim Fahy (RTE, 1991). Her son, Colonel Nick Hales Pakenham Mahon, was the commanding officer in the Grenadiers when Tom, Sue Attwood's husband, first joined them, remembered by them as kind to both subalterns and their young wives. Nick was stationed in Londonderry in the 1970s and was warned by the *Garda* not to live at Strokestown. He sold the property in 1979 to Jim Callery, a local businessman. The house and very fine gardens have been restored by him and his family; they are now open to the public, together with a Museum of the Irish Famine, based on the very extensive records of the house.
2. I can find no record of the house being damaged. It is true that Olive had done nothing wrong, but her great-grandfather, Major Denis Mahon, had been assassinated in 1847, in retaliation for his treatment of his tenants during the Famine, and the house had been left empty by the family until Olive's father had come back to live there in 1893.
3. The so-called Scramogue Ambush. Lieutenant John Harold Anthony Tennant, of Spofforth Grange, Harrogate, was killed in this ambush on 23 March, 1921, aged 21. Another officer was killed, and a Corporal seriously wounded. 'A disastrous affair': Sheppard, *The Ninth Lancers 1715–1936*, p. 311.
4. *Ibid.*, p. 310: 'an unhappy year … To describe it in detail would revive to no good purpose bitter memories best forgotten.'
5. In a long letter to his father, from the Army School of Education, Shorncliffe, he discusses the pros and cons of staying in the regiment and what to do if he

leaves. The main problem of staying is the expense of both sport and social life, especially polo and the Mess. Moreover, one is even 'judged by the dress of one's female friends … Barbara Goring's hunting kit was an offence for example!!!' Prospects are also slow, unless one has 'lots of push behind.' Yet India is not cheap either. 'Most fellows come home more or less in debt.' He also says that he is likely to want to marry 'by the time I am twenty-five or so', as he can no longer bear being on his own, after the companionship of the Army.

6. There were a few in the Second World War in Russia and the Far East.

Chapter 8

1. Kimberley is to the south-west of the Transvaal.
2. Cf. the Zulu word *umuTsha*, meaning loincloth.
3. Leopold Rosenbaum (1877–1952) was originally from Lithuania. He came to South Africa in 1893 and fought with the British in the Boer War. The other partner was L. H. Lax. They started Rosenbaum, Lax and Company in 1909. After the ostrich feather slump in 1914, they farmed lucerne and pioneered citrus-growing at Muden in Natal.

Chapter 10

1. London News Agency Photos Ltd. E. H. ('Toby') Wroughton and his brother were co-founders of the Davos English Ski Club in 1903, together with C. W. and E. C. Richardson. Toby was its first secretary (See chapter 1, note 5.)
2. All Cierva Autogiros were spelt thus, whereas 'autgyro, autogiro and gyroplane' referred to all other types of rotary-wing aircraft.
3. In April 1932, the Cierva Flying School actually charged £3 an hour for instruction. In 1935, it offered an 'A' licence training course from scratch for £35. Cf. Brie, *A History of British Rotorcraft 1866–1965* (1968), pp. 42–3 and Ord-Hume, *Juan de la Cierva and his Autogiros* (2011), p. 36.
4. Squadron Leader Henry Alan Marsh, AFC, AFRAeS (1901–50) and Wing Commander Reginald Alfred Charles Brie, MBE, FRAeS (1895–1989). In March 2018, the National Aerospace Library Sound Archive released an excellent interview with Reggie Brie, recorded in 1970, in which he describes his flying career, and his important role in promoting the use of the Autogiro, and later of the helicopter: aerosociety.com/podcast ('The Reggie Brie Interview'). This library also has the archive of photographs of Alan Marsh relating to his career as a pilot.
5. Cf. logbook for 28–29 August 1932: Hanworth to Walsall on the 28th, take-off and forced landing 9.15 on the 29th.
6. Squadron Leader Frederick John ('Jeep') Cable, AFC (1915–50). He was then aged only sixteen.
7. J. A. McMullen, MBE, was the author of *Simplified Aerial Navigation by Dead Reckoning* (1933), of which I have my father's copy. This was based on lectures given to RAF pupils in 1918, when 'about 100 flights were made to show pilots what could be done …' Evidently, he was then a very experienced airman, who as he says 'ceased to take much interest in aviation' after the War, but 'the recent great improvements in the Autogiro have induced him to become an owner-pilot, and that in spite of advancing years' (Preface, p. vi). The frontispiece shows him with his Autogiro. Apart from Cable, McMullen and Richardson, the first female soloist to qualify was Mrs J. G. Weir, and the

first female *ab initio* soloist was Mrs A. Jenkinson. By the end of 1932, eleven pupils had qualified: five women and six men. Cf. Brie, *A History of British Rotorcraft 1866–1965* (1968), p. 43.

8. Cf. Brooks, *Cierva Autogiros* (1988), p. 113: 'Adoption of Hanworth as the centre of Cierva's activities led to this attractive London airfield, with its then rural setting and country-house atmosphere, becoming the spiritual home of practical rotary-wing flight. There, up to World War Two, a band of enthusiasts, with all the zeal of early Christians, practised the cult and championed the cause of the Autogiro.'

9. The night flight from Croydon to Lympne was on 2 August 1933, between 12.30 and 1.15 a.m. (cf. logbook).

10. These trials actually took place in January 1935, on the deck of the *Fiume*. Cf. Brie, 'An Italian adventure', *in Aeronautics* (May 1959), pp. 22–7.

11. Cf. logbook for 28 April–18 May for flights by Jack in the C.24 (G-ABLM). This machine was built by de Havilland in 1931. It now belongs to the Science Museum, but it is on permanent loan to the de Havilland Aircraft Museum, Salisbury Hall, St Albans, where it is on display.

Chapter 11

1. Iain McNab ran the Grosvenor School of Modern Art at 33 Warwick Square, Pimlico, between 1925 and 1940. Lino-prints made by some artists there now sell for high prices. The Heatherley School of Fine Art was founded in 1845 and is now located in Lots Road, Chelsea.

2. Cf. logbook for 12 July 1935: solo demonstration for Maharajah of Patiala, five minutes, of C.30. Bhupinder Singh (1891–1938) was Maharaja of Patiala at this time, aged forty-four, and died three years later. He was the first Indian to own a car and an aircraft, and a keen cricketer. His older son, Yadavindra Singh (1913–74), was a first-class cricketer, and played in a test for India in 1934. Yet he was educated in Lahore. The younger son, Bhalindra Singh (1919–92), played one first-class match in England for Cambridge University in 1939. It was probably the older son, then aged twenty-two, who wanted to learn to fly an Autogiro. Later, the logbook records flights with a Mr Ghandi as passenger.

3. There was a National Coalition Government under Ramsay Macdonald at this time.

4. Hitler became chancellor of Germany on 30 January 1933. The purge known as the Night of the Long Knives took place between 30 June and 2 July 1934, and strengthened his power.

5. Hans-Wolfgang Herwarth von Bittenfeld (1871–1942).

6. Schloss Seerhausen is in Riesa Land, and was owned since 1729 by the Von Fritsch family. It is near Leipzig, but about 180 miles from Hanover. This does not fit the narrative. I conclude that it was at Leipzig that the pilots were met by the family chauffeur and taken to the castle, on 3 September, leaving on the 4th and going on to Cassel. The Logbook says 'stayed night 4th–5th at Seerhausen', but this was added later in different ink. They flew from Dessau to Leipzig, which is actually south of Dessau, and it only took thirty minutes of flying time. This only makes sense if they were going to stay that night with Hans' family. The castle is also quite near the Czech border. The last owner, Karl Alexander Hugo von Fritsch, with whom they stayed, took his own life in November 1945, after it was occupied by the Russians. They destroyed it in 1949. The stepchildren whom my father met were Hans (1898–1956)

and Renata (1908–82) Herwarth, children of Hans-Wolfgang Herwarth von Bittenfeld, by his first marriage to Katarina Wagenfuhr. They were divorced in 1914. Hans died in Stockbridge, Massachusetts, and Renata in Bern.

7. The card from Renata, with the dried carnation, is dated 4 September 1934 on the front, but on the back her note gives the 5th. She must have picked the flower on the day they left and posted the card next day. She writes: 'To commemorate Seerhausen and this "strange and dramatic family". Best wishes always, Renata Herwarth.' The card from her mother is dated the 11th and sent by post, in answer to a letter from my father. She also uses the same phrase, saying how happy the 'strange and dramatic family' was to see her son once more before leaving for the USA—'much too far from Seerhausen!' She adds: 'Please remember me to Mr. Malone and give him very many thanks for having been "the Swan" for our "Lohengrin". Weather simply beautiful these days, nearly tropical. Hoping of seeing you again one day. Very sincerely yours, Katarina v. Fritsch.' It is Hans who in his letter of 19 September to my father writes that he just received a message from his mother, saying how delighted they should be to see him again 'ANY TIME you should be in the vicinity of Seerhausen', and 'the same goes for Dick Malone, whom I just told that mother NEVER says what she does not mean. They really are quite dears, so if you can, give them the pleasure.'

8. The scrapbook has a map of the four attempted flights over the Pyrenees and a card from Mariano Martin, Fonda (inn), La Maruja, Boceguillas (Segovia), with note 'forced landing in Guadarama mountains'. This presumably identifies the village where they stayed the night. Cf. Robledo and Martin, *Boceguillas (1925–55)* (2010), pp. 46ff., for the Fonda La Maruja, Mariano Martin, and his family at this time. Pictures in this book show a very simple rural village. The owner of the Fonda installed the first septic tank. The priest at the time of the Civil War was called Don Alejandro (p. 48).

9. Cf. logbook: 6 January 1935 (Hanworth–Lympne–Berck–Villacoublay).

10. Cf. logbook: 10 January 1935 (by the same route).

11. Cf. logbook: 17–31 January 1935.

12. Cf. logbook: 14–30 June 1935.

Chapter 12

1. According to the official report, it took off in thick fog, veered off course, and hit the chimney of a house.

2. I have a copy of this (NJR). Two British MI6 officers, Cecil Bebb and Hugh Pollard, were involved in helping Franco to get away, as pilot and navigator of the plane. See also Preston, *The Spanish Civil War* (2006), p. 98. In a letter from my father to my mother dated 30 August 1936, he quotes a friend (Blake) as saying to him that the company is to reorganise and go to the public, but he doesn't know when, as 'Cierva is off his head just now, all his family in Spain in Red hands and is far too busy to think about any business, which must wait until he is calmer, if, that is, he isn't shot on one of his, frequent, absences from civilisation'.

Chapter 13

1. On the life of Hanna Reitsch cf. Mulley, *The Woman who Flew for Hitler* (2017).

2. Actually, these trips were before Cierva's death. Cf. logbook: 2–4 September and 4–10 October 1936. They are described in letters to my mother, who

was in Switzerland, of 2, 6, and 8 September, and 4 and 13 October. The first is written at the Imperial Hotel, Blackpool, where he was forced to spend a depressing night. Visibility was awful owing to low cloud and coastal fog. He had reached Kendal, some way further north, and then turned back. He says 'I don't like this lonely flying in murk and mist any more—once it was fun—now it only makes me feel a little unhappy—no excitement now—only wishing it was clear—hateful work'. He wonders 'if perhaps my nerves gone a bit?' He then reflects that pilots should be 'tough and unattached'. The second is from Clandeboye, where he was being kept from day to day 'as my host can't decide whether to keep his machine here or send me back with it'. The flight to Carlisle was 'rotten', but 'then clear sky and a heavenly evening and a following wind to blow me across'. He had a very good time with Lord Dufferin. The show was at Mount Stewart, home of Lord Londonderry, where he spent the whole afternoon flying solo or with passengers. As the weather was bad and it was 'a silly little field', the fixed-wing pilots were in trouble, and 'the giro was much in demand'. In the next days he watched the Ulster T. T. with Lord Dufferin and others, rode a horse, and 'attended Lady D. to church'. 'Feel much happier again about the flying—nerve has returned now completely I think.' Yet he longs to get back to Hanworth. 'My chief hardship is constantly refusing drinks in various quite too princely looking shapes and bottles. Hard to do but I dare not go out of control.' On 8 September, he writes from the ferry to Stranraer. The previous day 'was spent riding, being driven about at horrible speeds' in Lord Dufferin's new Bentley, walking round the woods and playing bridge. He was attracted by their dogs, a spaniel and a peke, and 'two pretty kids'. The second time he went to Belfast by night train on 1 October. On 4 October, he writes from Clandeboye: 'I'm dead tired from having flown half over Ireland, landed in unexpected places and ridden fierce horses all day.' He actually flew to Mulligan Strand and landed on the sands. On return (7–10 October) he had to fly Lord Dufferin from Liverpool to York Races in 'rather messy weather'. Dufferin had come over by airliner, my father bringing the Autogiro over via Carlisle. He then flew to Woodford near Manchester, stayed two nights with friends there, and returned to Hanworth on the 10th.

3. Cf. chapter 16 on radar calibration. For Autogiros in the Second World War, cf. also Brie, *A History of British Rotorcraft 1866–1965* (1968), pp. 45–6, 71ff.

Chapter 14

1. Ronald Macdonell was second in command of the regiment in May 1940 and took over command from June after the commanding officer was wounded. He was killed in September 1944. There is a tribute to him by Major General Norman in the introduction to Bright, *The Queen's Ninth Royal Lancers, 1936–45* (1951), p. xxvi: 'he was one of the best-loved Ninth Lancers of all time ... a rare combination of soldier and saint'.
2. On the Kandahar Club, see my father's poem '*K*'-*itis* in Appendix V.
3. 'Bill Bracken was undoubtedly the greatest ski-racer that ever represented Great Britain in international events', Lunn, *The Kandahar Story* (1969), p. 54.
4. The winner of the Parsenn Derby on the original course in 1931 was D. Zogg, with a time of thirteen minutes and forty-four seconds over a length of 10 kilometres and vertical fall of 1,400 metres.

5. Stuffy's father, A. J. C. Dowding, was headmaster of St Ninian's School, Moffat, the prep. school attended by E. C. Richardson, and presumably also by his brother, C. W. Richardson. So there was already a family connection. Stuffy Dowding was president of the Ski Club of Great Britain in 1924.

6. My father says that my mother never raced, but this is not true. On 10 January 1930, she won the Dôle Ski Club Challenge Shield at St Cergue, racing against some men—the first time a lady had won this race. The Club Journal says that they never thought a lady could win it. On 19 February that year she came sixth at Grindelwald in the Ladies' Ski Club Championship (slalom and straight race). On 26 January 1936, she was thirteenth in the Wengen Standard Course, in four minutes and 3.6 seconds, at an average speed of 21.2 mph. My father came fourth that day. She was also an experienced ski tourer. She skied down the Aletsch Glacier, i.e. from Konkordia Hut, to Morel in the Rhone Valley, in 1927, and there is a photo of her at the hut at Fuorcla Surlej, south of St Moritz, on a tour that evidently from the photos included the Roseg and Scerczen Glaciers. This probably took place after February 1928, since it is not included in her record of skiing experience dated 24 February that year, for her proposal as a member of the Ladies' Ski Club.

7. Owing to the political problem of Austria's support for Hitler, and the fact that Hannes Schneider had been imprisoned by the Nazis in 1938, the meeting was cancelled that year, and in 1939, it was called the Alpine-Kandahar. Lunn's father died on 18 March 1939.

8. I think I did hear it once. There is a report on the Alpine-Kandahar by Doreen Elliott in *British Ski Year Book* 10 (1939–41), pp. 173–9: 'Mr Lunn's unique knowledge and experience were badly missed on the Race Committee, and his polyglot speech at the prize-giving. We were grateful to Mr. J. W. Richardson for deputising at short notice' (p. 173). In the men's races the overall winner was Rominger from St Moritz, but the French were placed second, third, fourth, sixth, and seventh, with Couttet coming first in the straight race and second overall.

Chapter 15

1. For 1939–40, cf. Bright, *The Queen's Ninth Royal Lancers, 1936–45* (1951), introduction, xxii ff., and pp. 1–24. See also Appendix V, 'Record of service of Ninth Lancer officers', p. 317, for my father. The map facing p. 24 in Bright's book shows the movements of the Regiment in northern France, between Amiens and Rouen. There is another on p. 73 of *The Diary of a Staff Officer* (London, 1941), on which my father has marked their routes, and one in his scrapbook. For the broader picture, cf. Horne, *To Lose a Battle: France 1940* (2007).

2. For a vivid first-hand account, cf. Neave, *The Flames of Calais* (1972).

3. Cf. Bright, *op. cit.* p. 2, 'It was decided that Armour no longer needed artillery support', and pp. 3–5 on the 'appalling lack of readiness' of the regiment and the failure to give them infantry or air support.

4. On 23–24 May, to Hornoy-le-Bourg, arriving at 7 a.m. on the 24th.

5. The first attack on Abbeville was on the 27th, by the Bays and Tenth Hussars, with the Ninth Lancers in reserve. It was a total failure with heavy losses.

6. Yet on the 28–29th the Ninth Lancers successfully attacked, together with a French division led by De Gaulle, and captured Bailleul and Limeux, south-west of Abbeville. They were able to make a tour of the battlefield

afterwards, and were sent a personal message from the general officer commanding on the 31st, praising them, and stressing the importance of their attempt to cross the Somme, as vital to the British Expeditionary Force. On the 30th, they were re-formed into a new Composite Regiment, with the Fifty-first Highland Division. They moved south-west of the river Bresle on 1 June to St Léger-aux-Bois, as a mobile reserve.

7. Calais fell on 26 May, and the evacuation of Dunkirk was completed by 3 June. From 4 June, the regiment was engaged in a series of actions near Le Tréport and Eu, along the Bresle, and subsequently further south-west, down to Forêt de Lyons east of Rouen, until on 8–9 June, they were withdrawn across the Seine, before the Pont de L'Arche was blown. There followed a long withdrawal, via Surville and Le Mans, where on the 13th 'some people even found time to fish in the moat around the chateau, though without success'. Cf. Bright *op. cit.*, p. 22. We still have the fishing rod my father took with him to France, which I used to use. Evacuation was ordered by Viscount Alanbrooke on the 15th.

8. Cf. Bright, *op. cit.*, p. 23. They embarked on the *Lady of Man*, which was already full. There were over 2,000 men on board. She arrived at Plymouth at dawn on 17 June, the day on which the French surrendered.

Chapter 16

1. Cf. letter of 8 August 1942 to my father from Major General Ward, US Army, Commanding: 'Thank you for your excellent liaison work between the 82nd Group and the 1st Armoured Division during "Defiance". The work of the Air Support was efficient and very much appreciated by us. It was the best I have ever seen.'

2. For a good account of radar calibration, in which Brie and Marsh played leading parts, cf. Elizabeth Brie, 'Battle of Britain anniversary: the Autogiro and radar', *Helicopter International* (2010), pp. 46–7.

3. Cf. letter of 2 February 1943 from Crawford to my father: 'I was very interested to learn of your experience with Rotating Wing Aircraft. Since coming to the War Office I have taken up the question of Rotating Wing Aircraft and hope that we shall soon get some Helicopters from America … I will bear you in mind if and when we get to the state of practical development.'

4. Cf. letter of 4 September 1943 from a brigadier (Air) to War Office, about the grant of the Army Flying Badge: 'it would appear that the circumstances require that this application should be given consideration as a special case.'

Chapter 17

1. He wrote several reports to the War Office between January and May 1944.

2. In his report to the War Office of April 1945, my father says that about forty R.4 Sikorskys had arrived in the UK towards the end of 1944, and were being used for training purposes by the Navy and Air Ministry. Two R.4s had already been brought over from the States in January 1944 by Brie and Cable. These crossed the Atlantic on shipboard, and were then flown to Hanworth. A large order was placed for the more developed Sikorsky R.5 model, but these were never sent. It is presumably the R.5 to which he is referring here. His Logbook records that he flew several of the R.4s between November 1944 and February 1945.

3. Cf. the certificate in the scrapbook, dated 11 April 1944, to certify that 'Major J. W. Richardson, British Army, has satisfactorily completed the course of instruction in flying the Sikorsky YR-4 helicopter and has been checked-out as being a fully competent solo pilot on that aircraft'.

Chapter 18

1. Cf. Reports to the War Office, April 1945.
2. The current world speed record for a helicopter is 249.10 mph, with a Westland Lynx.
3. This was the Air Horse. Cf. Brie, *A History of British Rotorcraft 1866–1965* (1968), pp. 87-90, Ord-Hume, *Juan de la Cierva and his Autogiros* (2011), pp. 78–9.
4. The letter from Lt General Crawford, dated 2 April 1946, describes the duties carried out by Major Richardson between 1941 and 1946, and ends: 'Maj Richardson has shown ability and great tenacity of purpose in carrying out these duties. His reports to the War Office on the whole problem of Helicopters have been of great value and have provided much of the material on which the future policy of the Army will be based with regard to Rotary Wing Aircraft.'

Chapter 19

1. 'Examination of the Case for a London Heliport' (January 1958). Reggie Brie also played an important part in this campaign.

Appendix I

1. Much of the following information is taken from the work of Kitty Richardson, my father's cousin, especially her *Richardsons: A Family History* (1992) and *Richardsons: A Business History* (1992).
2. Cf. Duffy, *Fight for a Throne: the Jacobite '45 Reconsidered* (2015), pp. 362 and 369.
3. *Travels along the Mediterranean and parts adjacent in company of the Earl of Belmore* (1822).
4. *London Quarterly Review* (October 1822), p. 61.
5. *Conversations of Lord Byron with the Countess of Blessington* (1893), pp. 330–33.
6. *Ski Notes and Queries* (May 1954), p. 24.
7. *British Ski Year Book* (1939–41), pp. 396–7.
8. *Journal of Genetics* No. 3 (1914), pp. 171–7; No. 7 (1918), pp. 167–70; No. 10 (1920), pp. 39–46; and No. 13 (1923), pp. 147–52.
9. On the contribution of the two brothers to skiing and ski jumping see also Ashburner, *The History of Ski Jumping* (2003), and Collard, *The Snow Queen's Magic Gown: the lost world of the pioneer ski-runners, 1860–1914* (2007).

Appendix II

1. On the Lancashire Landing cf. Hart, *Gallipoli* (2013), pp. 132–8.
2. *The British and Foreign Confectioner* (1 December 1877).
3. Lauder, *Memorial of the Royal Progress in Scotland* (c. 1842).

Appendix III

1. He died in October–December 1902 in London. Vyvien was born on 21 June 1884, so she should have been eighteen then.
2. She is listed as being at the Slade in 1901–2 and 1903, living at 37 Warrington Crescent.
3. 1902 or 1903 to 1908.
4. The dressmaker was very probably Ada Nettleship, the wife of the artist Jack Nettleship, whose daughter Ida married Augustus John. Cf. John and Holroyd, *The Good Bohemian. The Letters of Ida John*, pp. 1–2, 6–7, and *passim*. According to them Ada 'embodied the puritan culture of the Victorians'. Jack's pictures did not sell and Ada earned the money for the family. Her team of girls worked hard and for long hours. She had a quick temper, and an authoritative personality. The family was also friendly with the Salamans, who lived on Mill Hill, near the Bishops. Louise Salaman married Henry Bishop's son Edgar William.
5. Her first child was John Anthony Vyvien Hart-Davis, born 26 April 1910.
6. Richard Hugh was born on 14 September 1914.
7. She was sunk on 7 May 1915.
8. The 1st Battalion Lancashire Fusiliers actually landed on W Beach (Tekke Bay), the famous 'Lancashire Landing', commanded by Colonel Harry Bishop: cf. Appendix II.
9. Hussein Ibn Ali al-Hashimi (1853/4–1931) was sharif and emir of Mecca from 1908 and king of the Hejaz 1916–24. He started the Arab Revolt against the Ottoman Empire in 1916 but was forced to go into exile in 1924 in Cyprus by the Saudi family. He died in Amman in 1931, where his son, Abdullah, was king.
10. Probably Faisal of Iraq and Abdullah of Transjordan.
11. This may refer to the Arab Kingdom of Syria, which lasted from March to July 1920.
12. Vyvien does not name her children in these memoirs. Her older son was John Anthony Vyvien Hart-Davis, born in Fiji (see note 5). He became an electrical engineer, and worked for GEC. He married Elaine Murray Tosh (born 1912) on 20 July 1935. Before the war, they lived in Hong Kong. John was captured there by the Japanese, and was in a prison camp in Japan. He died in 1994. John and Elaine's first daughter, Prudence, was born on 26 January 1938. During the War she was evacuated with her mother to Canada. They returned to England in 1944 on a banana boat via the Arctic. Prue was in the RAF, and married John W. Hardie in 1964. Her children are Alison Gail Hardie (born 1974) and Graeme Mchallum Hardie (born 1976). Graeme married Nicola Humphries on 9 May 2013, and they have two sons, Callum and Mikey. John Hardie died in 2015.
     John Hart-Davis' second daughter is Victoria, born in 1947. She married Derek C. Evans in 1976, and later John Kidney. Her children are Benjamin Charles Elmslie Evans (born 1 October 1978) and Laura Victoria Powell (born 22 April 1982).
     Vyvien's second son Richard Hugh Hart-Davis was born in Fiji (see note 6). He served in the war with the East African Rifles. He was not married and died in 2002.
     Vyvien's daughter was Ann Elizabeth Hart-Davis. She was born on 21 March 1920. She married Edwin S. Taylor in 1945, then James S. Pyper in 1956. She died on 27 February 2003. She and Hugh both lived in Nether Stowey, their parents' home village, for much of the later part of their lives.

Appendix IV

1. Richardson, *Richardsons: A Family History* (1992), p. 87.
2. Bennett, *Seahorse* (2005), p. 160.

Bibliography

Allcard, C., *A Gypsy Life* (New York and London: Norton, 1992; third edition, Bognor Regis: Imperator Publishing, 2016)

Ashburner, T., *The History of Ski Jumping* (Shrewsbury: Quiller Press, 2003)

Barnes, M. (ed.), *Curtis Moffat: Silver Society* (Göttingen: Steidl in association with V & A Publishing, 2016)

Bennett, C. S., *Seahorse! Between the Sea and the Saddle* (Tiverton: Halsgrove, 2005)

Bell, C. M., *Churchill and the Dardanelles* (Oxford: Oxford University Press, 2017)

Bishop, H. O. M., *One Young Soldier: The Memoirs of a Cavalryman*, edited by Bruce Shand (Norwich: Michael Russell, 1993)

Brie, E., 'Battle of Britain anniversary: The Autogiro and radar', *Helicopter International* (2010), pp. 46–7

Brie, R., *The Autogiro and how to Fly it* (London: Pitman, second edition, 1935)

Brie, R.A. C., 'An Italian adventure', *Aeronautics* (May 1959), pp. 22–7

Brie, R. A. C., *A History of British Rotorcraft 1866–1965* (Yeovil: Westland Helicopters Ltd., 1968)

Bright, J., *The Queen's Ninth Royal Lancers 1936–45* (Aldershot: Gale and Polden, 1951)

British Ski Year Book 10 (1939–41)

Brooks, P. W., *Cierva Autogiros: The Development of Rotary-Wing Flight* (Shrewsbury: Airlife Publishing Ltd., 1988)

Byron, George Gordon, Lord, and Blessington, Marguerite, Countess of, *Conversations of Lord Byron with the Countess of Blessington* (London: Bentley, 1894?)

Collard, J. M., *The Snow Queen's Magic Gown: the lost world of the pioneer ski-runners, 1860–1914* (London: published by the author, 2007)

Crichton Somerville, D. M. M., Rickmers, W. R., and Richardson, E. C., *Ski-running* (London: Horace Cox, 1904)

Duffy, C., *Fight for a Throne: the Jacobite '45 Reconsidered* (Solihull: Hellion and Co., 2015)

Harding, M. D., *Air-Bird in the Water: The Life and Works of Pearl Craigie (John Oliver Hobbes)*, (Madison, NJ: Farleigh Dickinson University Press, 1996)

Hart, P., *Gallipoli* (London: Profile Books, paperback edition, 2013)

Hart-Davis, V. C., *Personal Reminiscences, Gold Coast, Fiji, Cyprus* (Bodleian MSS. Brit. Emp. S. 346)

Hone, J., *The Life of Henry Tonks* (London: Heinemann, 1939)

Horne, A., *To Lose a Battle: France 1940* (London: Penguin, 2007)

John, R. and Holroyd, M., *The Good Bohemian. The Letters of Ida John* (London: Bloomsbury, 2017)

Lauder, Sir T. D., *Memorial of the Royal Progress in Scotland* (Edinburgh: 1843)

Marsh, J. B., *Steephill Castle, Ventnor, Isle of Wight: the residence of John Morgan Richards, Esq.; a handbook and a history* (London: Dangerfield Printing Company, 1907)

McMullen, J. A., *Simplified Aerial Navigation by Dead Reckoning* (London: Charles Griffin and Company, 1933)

Mulley, C., *The Woman who flew for Hitler* (London: Macmillan, 2017)

Neave, A., *The Flames of Calais: A Soldier's Battle* (London: Hodder and Stoughton, 1972)

Ord-Hume, A. W. G., *Juan de la Cierva and his Autogiros* (Catrine, Ayrshire: Stenlake, 2011)

Ormond, P. S., *The Basques and their Country* (London: Simpkin, Marshall, Hamilton, Kent and Co., second edition, 1926)

Preston, P., *The Spanish Civil War: Reaction, Revolution and Revenge* (London: Harper Perennial, 2006)

Rabutin, M., 'Le Salon d'Automne de 1904', *La Revue Libre* 7 (Novembre 1904), pp. 213–4

Richards, J. M., *Almost Fairyland* (London, John Hogg, 1914)

Richardson, C. W., 'A preliminary note on the genetics of Fragaria', *Journal of Genetics* 3, no. 3 (1914), pp. 171–7

Ditto, 'A further note on the genetics of Fragaria', *Journal of Genetics* 7, no. 3 (1918), pp. 167–70

Ditto, 'Some notes on Fragaria (with two text figures), *Journal of Genetics* 10, no. 1 (1920), pp. 39–46

Ditto, 'Notes on Fragaria', *Journal of Genetics* 13, no. 2 (1923), pp. 147–52

Richardson, E. C., *The ski-runner* (London: The Author, 1909)

Richardson, K. M., *Richardsons: A Family History* (Edinburgh: privately printed, 1992); *Richardsons: A Business History* (Edinburgh: privately printed, 1992)

Richardson, R., *Travels along the Mediterranean and parts adjacent in company of the Earl of Belmore during the years 1816–17–18, extending as far as the Second Cataract of the Nile, Jerusalem, Damascus, Balbec, etc.* (London: Cadell, and Edinburgh: Blackwood, 1822)

Robledo, M. A. and Martin, A. de D., *Boceguillas (1925–55)* (Madrid: Aebius, 2010)

Shakespeare, N., *Six Minutes in May. How Churchill unexpectedly became Prime Minister* (London: Harvill Secker, 2017)

Sheppard, E. W., *The Ninth Lancers 1715–1936* (Aldershot: Gale and Polden, 1939)

Ski Notes and Queries (May 1954)

The British and Foreign Confectioner (1 December 1877)

The Davos Courier (31 January 1902)

The Diary of a Staff Officer (London: Methuen, third edition, 1941)

Uttley, M. R. H., *Westland and the British Helicopter Industry 1945–60* (London: Routledge, 2013)